CALORIC®
Oven Magic
Cookbook

A Benjamin Company Book

Project Manager: William Day
Project Coordinator: Beth Kukkonen
Home Economist: Martha S. Reynolds
Editor: Barbara Bloch
Production Manager: Patricia Drew
Production Assistants: Florence Colarusso, Virginia Schomp,
                                Peter Wilson
Photography: Robert Buchanan
Typography: A-Line, Milwaukee

Precautions to avoid possible exposure to excessive microwave energy:

(a) DO NOT attempt to operate this oven with the door open since open door operation can result in harmful exposure to microwave energy. It is important not to defeat or tamper with the safety interlocks.

(b) DO NOT place any object between the oven front face and the door or allow soil or cleaner residue to accumulate on sealing surfaces.

(c) DO NOT operate the oven if it is damaged. It is particularly important that the oven door close properly and that there is no damage to the: (1) Door (bent), (2) hinges and latches (broken or loosened), (3) door seals and sealing surfaces.

(d) The oven should not be adjusted or repaired by anyone except properly qualified service personnel.

Prepared and produced by The Benjamin Company, Inc.
One Westchester Plaza
Elmsford, New York 10523

ISBN: 0-87502-104-2
Library of Congress Card Catalog Number: 82-072357

Printed in the United States of America
First Printing: October, 1982

TABLE OF CONTENTS

The History
Of
Caloric

In Philadelphia, back in 1899, Samuel Klein founded Klein Stove Company, to manufacture wood-burning and coal-burning stoves. His modest start established the base for what was to become The Caloric Corporation, one of the country's leading designers, manufacturers, and marketers of modern cooking appliances.

The iron forges and foundries of Topton, famous from the days of the colonists and the Revolutionary War, provided the necessary cast iron parts for Klein's stoves. From the heart of the Pennsylvania Dutch Country, shipments rolled by wagon and train to the plant in Philadelphia.

Early in its development, the company began specializing in gas-burning ranges. In 1903, the company was identified with the word "Caloric," derived from the Latin *calor*, which means "heat."

Caloric grew and prospered. During World War I it acquired the old Topton Foundry and Machine Company. Soon there were three separate manufacturing locations in Pennsylvania. By 1941, however, all operations had been centralized at the site of the old foundry in Topton. The foundry itself was finally closed in 1968 when Caloric became the first major stove manufacturer to eliminate cast iron components in gas ranges.

Since mid-century, Caloric has grown substantially and has established itself as a leading innovator in the appliance field. Among its contributions to "state of the art" technology have been many "firsts." They include: the patented Ultra-Ray infra-red radiant broiler; the gas pyrolytic self-cleaning oven; automatic pilotless ignition; and the full-power microwave common cavity electric and gas ranges.

Caloric had a long and exclusive association with gas ranges, but since 1972 it has been producing major electric cooking centers to go along with the gas appliances. There is now a complete line of ranges and cooking centers, both conventional and microwave, along with other kitchen appliances such as dishwashers, trash compactors, and food disposers.

Since 1966, Caloric has been part of the Raytheon Company. It has continued to expand and broaden its product line. In 1978 Caloric acquired the Glenwood Range Company, a manufacturer of quality appliances in the economy and middle price categories. The Modern Maid Company joined the Caloric family in 1981, bringing with it the capacity for manufacturing high quality built-in ovens and cooktops.

Caloric is dedicated to the development and improvement of quality kitchen appliances. The resources and talents of the company are constantly and devotedly directed to the goal of making life easier and more pleasant for the American family.

Your
Caloric Range
and
How It Works

Caloric's "ME" Range, whether gas or electric, is designed to cook with the incredible speed and convenience of microwave energy, the traditional method of cooking by heat, or both, in the same oven cavity. As you learn to use your new range, you'll discover the exciting features of this appliance. This revolutionary cooking center gives you the choice of cooking by three different methods — by heat, by microwave energy, or by a combination of heat and microwave energy at the same time.

The electric "ME" Range features **radiant heat cooking** or **variable power microwave cooking,** or **both simultaneously.** No special new techniques are necessary when you use the electric oven to bake or broil. You'll find your new oven is well insulated, which helps food cook evenly, keeps your kitchen cool, and lowers the cost of operation. This oven is self-cleaning.

The "ME" Gas Range features **gas convection cooking, variable power microwave cooking,** or **both simultaneously.** Convection cooking uses forced hot air. When the convection oven is on, air is heated by a gas burner behind the back wall of the oven. Two powerful fans circulate the hot air in the oven and around the food. The hot air is recirculated and kept at a constant temperature. This forced circulation of hot air around the food is so efficient that cooking can be accomplished at lower temperatures than in a traditional radiant heat oven. When trying your own recipes in the convection oven, we suggest you reduce the oven temperature setting by 50°F. Usually, convection ovens don't need to be preheated because the fans circulate the hot air in the oven quickly and heat it to baking temperature in just 3 or 4 minutes. This oven is also self-cleaning.

All the recipes in this book have been tested in all cooking methods. Timing is affected greatly by starting temperature. Therefore, recipes have been tested assuming normal storage temperature of the particular food. You can choose the cooking method that best fits your needs. You may prefer one method for some food and a different one for others. Every recipe in the book has five symbols. The pages that follow show you these symbols and describe the special characteristics and advantages of each.

THE SYMBOLS

If you have a "ME" Gas Range, you have a choice of cooking by gas convection, microwave, or combination (combo) gas convection and microwave. If you have an electric "ME" Range, you have a choice of cooking by radiant electric, microwave, or combination (combo) radiant electric and microwave. You will note that the microwave method is the same for both the gas and electric ranges.

This symbol indicates the gas convection method. This is the method that uses circulating hot air. You'll note that temperature settings are about 50°F lower than you might be used to, for cooking in approximately the same length of time. If the oven must be preheated, 3 to 4 minutes, rather than 10 minutes, is all you need. Occasionally, you will find that recipes require rotating during the cooking time. To make food brown more evenly, rotate dishes one-half turn, halfway through cooking.

This symbol indicates electric radiant heat. Most recipes in cookbooks and magazines are prepared this way. There is no special trick or technique to cooking by this method. Referring to this method will help you to convert your own recipes to any other cooking method you desire.

This symbol indicates combination (combo) cooking by gas convection and microwave at the same time. The incredible speed of the microwave and the efficiency of circulating hot air team up for fast results and splendid appearance. Food cooks in one-quarter to one-half the conventional cooking time. Because it's fast and the cooking temperature is lower, you'll use less energy. However, food requiring browning may need to be cooked 25°F to 50°F higher than in the straight gas convection method.

This symbol indicates combination (combo) cooking by electric radiant and microwave at the same time. The amazing speed of the microwave and radiant heat produce fast and beautiful results. Food cooks in one-quarter to one-half the conventional time. Temperature settings are usually 25°F to 50°F higher than in straight electric radiant cooking due to the speed of the microwave. You'll still use less energy because the time needed is shorter.

This symbol indicates microwave cooking, the fastest cooking method available today. Food heats by vibrating waves of energy. These waves penetrate the food from the outside toward the center. The waves cause the molecules of the food to vibrate. This vibration causes heat which cooks the food. Because food cooks so quickly, many foods do not brown, and crisp crusts do not form. In cooking, there are many factors which influence the amount of time needed to cook food. This is even more true in microwave cooking. Starting temperature, quantity, density, and the shape of food are important considerations. The moisture, sugar and fat content of food will also affect cooking time. Larger quantities take longer to cook than smaller. Thick chunks of meat need more time than thinner slices. Denser foods need more time than lighter ones. (A steak, for instance, will not cook as quickly as the same amount of ground meat.) Microwave energy is attracted to sugar and fat in food. Foods containing

YOUR CALORIC RANGE AND HOW IT WORKS

these substances will heat more rapidly than foods containing a large amount of water.

As a rule, it is wise to cook food for less time than you think is needed, test for doneness, and if necessary, continue to cook a few seconds or minutes longer.

SPECIAL MICROWAVE HINTS AND TIPS

NEVER turn the oven on when it is empty. There should always be at least a glass of water in the oven when it is operating in the microwave method.

Cover food lightly with a sheet of waxed paper during cooking to contain heat and reduce splatters.

When using plastic wrap as a cover, be sure to turn back a corner and leave a vent for steam to escape. We recommend that only SARAN WRAP® be used for covering in the microwave method.

Do not use waxed paper or plastic wrap if there is heat in the oven cavity.

Whenever possible, place food in a round container or circular pattern with the thickest part of the food toward the outer edge of the dish.

Pierce food that has a skin around it. Food such as egg yolks, chicken livers, hard-shell squash, and potatoes could erupt in the oven if they are not pierced.

For more even cooking, food may need to be turned over, stirred, or rearranged during microwave cooking time.

UTENSILS

Metal utensils reduce microwave effiency and should not be used when cooking by microwave power alone. Metal pans reflect microwave energy rather than allowing it to pass through. Use heat proof glass or china without metal trim. Paper plates, plastics that are microwave safe, paper towels, plastic bags, styrofoam cups, and almost any non-metal container are also recommended for microwave use. Many new microwave baking utensils especially designed for microwave cooking are available. Many of these are heat resistant as well and may be used in the combination oven. If you are not sure whether or not a utensil is microwave safe, test it by placing a glass measure of water next to the utensil in the oven. Cook at 100% microwave power 2 minutes. If the utensil is hot, it is not microwave safe. If it is cool, the container may be used for microwave cooking.

Metal pans which should not be used in microwave cooking alone may be used in combination cooking. Although the microwaves cannot penetrate the metal, the heat cooks the food directly in contact with the metal surface of the pan. You'll note that glass and metal pans give slightly different results. Since glass utensils allow the microwave energy to pass through, food will cook slightly faster than in metal pans. Food appearance will be about the same in either pan.

Some utensils that are safe in microwave cooking should not be used in combination cooking. These include plastic wrap, waxed paper, plastic containers, paper plates and cups, styrofoam, and meat thermometers (both conventional and microwave). However, Caloric has developed a thin stemmed thermometer which is safe to use in both microwave and combination cooking.

When using the convection method, use shallow pans whenever possible. This allows the hot air to surround the food more evenly. A ceramic broiler pan has been supplied with the "ME" Gas Range. The design of this pan enables you to broil without turning the food.

PREHEATING

A preheated oven may or may not be necessary. The length of time food needs to be cooked will determine whether or not you should preheat your oven. Food such as cookies, cakes, or breads should always be cooked in a preheated oven. You should preheat when cooking time is short to be sure there is ample enough heat in the oven to brown the food properly. When using the electric radiant or gas convection methods, you will not need to preheat very often. When using the combination methods, we sometimes recommend preheating. This is due to the speed with which food cooks in these methods.

RACK POSITION

For most cooking, the oven rack with the ceramic cooking shelf should be used in the second rack position from the bottom. This position insures even cooking and constant results. For broiling, the rack with the ceramic cooking shelf should be placed in the fourth position from the bottom in the electric oven. For longer broiling times, it may be necessary to lower the rack in the oven.

The ceramic cooking shelf in the center of the oven rack is there for your convenience. It enables you to place small items, such as custard cups or coffee cups, in the oven.

RECIPE CONVERSION

You probably have some favorite family recipes which you'd like to try to convert to a different cooking method than the conventional one you are used to. Below are a few tips to help you do this.

To convert to the microwave method: Start by reducing the liquid by one-third. Liquid must usually be reduced because the microwave oven does not have heat which will evaporate the liquid as quickly as in a conventional oven. Reduce cooking time by one-quarter the original time, test for doneness, and if necessary, continue to cook.

To convert to the gas convection method: Reduce baking temperature by 50°F. Set the time as your recipe directs. Check about halfway through and rotate the dish one-half turn if food appears to be browning unevenly. Test for doneness as usual.

To convert to the combination methods: Combination cook at 75% microwave power and 25°F higher in the electric combination method or 25°F lower in the gas convection combination method. Check for doneness after one-third the cooking time. Most food is cooked by

YOUR CALORIC RANGE AND HOW IT WORKS

combination (combo) for the entire cooking time. Some food, such as breads, cakes, and pies, should be baked first and combination cooked last so that the food has time to cook to its proper consistency. Other foods, such as roasts, casseroles, or appetizers, should be combination cooked first and baked last for quick cooking and browning.

Recipe conversions will become easier as you become familiar with your new oven. You will find it helpful to look through this book and find a recipe similar to the one you wish to convert. Look at the electric method first. Then check the method which you wish to convert to. Make the same time, temperature, and microwave power adjustments as the book does. Check for doneness a few minutes before the time will be up. You can always cook additional time if it is needed.

TO CONVERT A RECIPE

Your recipe calls for a 325°F oven for 25 minutes.

To cook gas convection: Cook at 275°F for 25 minutes.

To cook microwave: Cook at 75% power 7½ minutes.

To cook electric radiant and microwave combination: Cook at 350°F and 50% microwave power 8 minutes.

To cook gas convection and microwave combination: Cook at 300°F and 50% microwave power 8 minutes.

A FEW FINAL CONVERSION TIPS

For additional browning, increase temperature slightly.

For food that needs to cook slowly to achieve tenderness, use lower microwave power (40% to 50%).

Increase microwave power to cook food more quickly.

Cook combination 25°F higher than you would conventionally.

CLEANING YOUR OVEN

When you clean the oven, place the ceramic cooking shelf and the Microdome® in the oven during the self-cleaning cycle. Remove the wire racks during the cycle and clean them by hand. The wire racks will discolor if they are not removed from the oven. Refer to the owner's guide for complete instructions.

Tempting Tidbits

Stuffed Mushrooms _____ 24 appetizers

24 medium-size mushrooms
1½ ounces cream cheese (half
　　of 3-ounce package),
　　at room temperature
½ cup chopped walnuts
⅓ cup shredded Cheddar
　　cheese
¼ cup finely chopped fresh
　　parsley
2 tablespoons minced
　　scallion
½ teaspoon salt
1 clove garlic, minced

Wipe mushrooms with damp paper towel and carefully remove stems. (Reserve stems for use at another time.) Place mushrooms, rounded side down, in 8 × 12-inch baking dish.* Combine cream cheese, walnuts, Cheddar cheese, parsley, scallion, salt, and garlic. Spoon into mushrooms.

 Preheat oven to 375°F. Combo cook at 75% microwave power and 375°F 5 minutes, or until mushrooms are tender and filling is set.

 Preheat oven to 325°F. Bake 10 to 12 minutes until mushrooms are tender and filling is set.

 Preheat oven to 425°F. Combo cook at 75% microwave power and 425°F 5 minutes, or until mushrooms are tender and filling is set.

 Preheat oven to 375°F. Bake 10 to 12 minutes until mushrooms are tender and filling is set.

 Cook at 50% microwave power 8 to 9 minutes until mushrooms are tender and filling is set.

* In microwave method, be sure to use a microwave safe baking dish.

Cocktail Quiches _____ 24 quiches

Pastry for 1-crust 9-inch
    pie (page 158)
⅓ cup minced cooked shrimp,
    flaked crab meat, or
    drained caviar
⅔ cup heavy cream
 2 eggs, beaten
 2 teaspoons chopped fresh
    dill
 2 tablespoons sliced
    scallion
½ teaspoon salt

Roll out pastry very thin and cut into rounds with 2¾-inch cookie cutter. Fit into twenty-four 1¾-inch muffin cups. (In microwave method, pre-cook pastry as directed below.) Spoon ½ teaspoon shrimp into each pastry-lined muffin cup. Blend cream, eggs, dill, scallion, and salt until smooth. Spoon over shrimp.

 Preheat oven to 400°F. Total Cooking Time: 15 minutes. Combo cook at 75% microwave power and 400°F 3 minutes. Bake at 400°F 12 additional minutes, or until filling is set and pastry is browned.

 Preheat oven to 350°F. Bake 20 to 25 minutes until filling is set and pastry is browned, rotating once.

 Preheat oven to 450°F. Total Cooking Time: 15 minutes. Combo cook at 75% microwave power and 450°F 3 minutes. Bake at 450°F 12 additional minutes, or until filling is set and pastry is browned.

 Preheat oven to 400°F. Bake 20 to 25 minutes until filling is set and pastry is browned.

 Preheat oven to 375°F. Bake unfilled pastry 12 to 15 minutes until lightly browned. Cool. Remove from metal muffin cups and place on microwave safe plate. Fill as directed above. Cook at 100% microwave power 2½ to 3 minutes until filling is set.

Bacon Wrapped Appetizers — 24 appetizers

12 slices bacon, cut in half
3 chicken livers, cut in half
6 oysters
4 water chestnuts
1 egg white
1 teaspoon Dijon mustard
4 mushrooms
4 ½-inch chunks zucchini
⅔ cup fresh bread crumbs (toasted in microwave method)

Wrap a piece of bacon around each chicken liver half, oyster, and water chestnut. (In microwave method, pre-cook bacon as directed below.) Secure with wooden toothpick. Beat egg white, mustard, and 1 teaspoon water until smooth. Dip mushrooms and zucchini in mustard mixture. Coat mushrooms and zucchini with bread crumbs and wrap each with a piece of bacon. Secure with wooden toothpick.

MICROWAVE FIRST

Place rack in 4th position from bottom. Preheat broiler 3 minutes. Arrange appetizers on rack set over broiler pan. Total Cooking Time: 7 minutes. Combo cook at 75% microwave power and 450°F 4 minutes. Broil 3 additional minutes, or until bacon is lightly browned and crisp.

Place rack in 4th position from bottom. Preheat broiler 3 minutes. Arrange appetizers on rack set over broiler pan. Broil 7 to 9 minutes until bacon is lightly browned and crisp.

MICROWAVE FIRST

Place rack in 4th position from bottom. Preheat broiler 3 minutes. Arrange appetizers on broiler pan. Total Cooking Time: 6 minutes. Combo cook at 75% microwave power and broil 4 minutes. Broil 2 additional minutes, or until bacon is lightly browned and crisp.

Place rack in 4th position from bottom. Preheat broiler 3 minutes. Arrange appetizers on broiler pan. Broil 8 minutes, or until bacon is lightly browned and crisp, turning once.

Place bacon on paper towel. Cover with another paper towel and cook at 100% microwave power 3 minutes. Assemble appetizers as directed above. Arrange appetizers on 2 microwave safe plates. Cook at 100% microwave power 4 minutes, or until livers and bacon are cooked.

Baked Brie ———————————— 6 to 8 servings

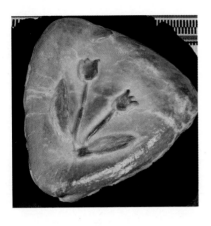

1 package (8 ounces)
   refrigerator crescent
   rolls
1 wedge Brie cheese (½
   to ¾ pound)
1 egg yolk
1 tablespoon milk

Separate crescent dough into 4 rectangles. Make 2 squares by overlapping long edges of 2 rectangles. Press seam firmly and pinch perforations to seal. Roll out each square into a rectangle 1 inch larger all around than the cheese. Place cheese on one dough rectangle. Fold dough up over cut edges and rounded back edge of cheese. Trim dough to fit; reserve trimmings. Beat egg yolk and milk. Brush some of the yolk mixture generously over sides of dough. Place other dough rectangle on top of cheese and press lightly around egg-brushed edges to seal. Trim dough close to bottom edge of cheese. Place on greased baking sheet. Brush generously with some of the yolk mixture. Cut decorations from trimmings. Arrange on top and brush with remaining yolk mixture.

Preheat oven to 375°F. Total Cooking Time: 10 to 12 minutes. Combo cook at 50% microwave power and 375°F 4 minutes. Bake at 375°F 6 to 8 additional minutes until well browned. Let stand 10 minutes. Place on cheese board to serve.

Preheat oven to 325°F. Bake 15 minutes, or until well browned. Let stand 10 minutes. Place on cheese board to serve.

Preheat oven to 425°F. Total Cooking Time: 10 to 12 minutes. Combo cook at 50% microwave power and 425°F 4 minutes. Bake at 425°F 6 to 8 additional minutes until well browned. Let stand 10 minutes. Place on cheese board to serve.

Preheat oven to 375°F. Bake 15 to 18 minutes until well browned. Let stand 10 minutes. Place on cheese board to serve.

Not recommended.

Baked Cheese Bites _____ 32 appetizers

½ pound mozzarella, Swiss,
  Jarlsberg, fontina, or
  similar firm cheese
1 cup dry bread crumbs
½ teaspoon oregano
¼ teaspoon salt
2 eggs, beaten

Cut cheese into thirty-two ½- to ¾-inch cubes. Combine bread crumbs, oregano, and salt. Dip cubes in eggs, then in crumb mixture, coating each cube twice. Place on lightly greased baking sheet.* Let stand a few minutes to dry before cooking.

Preheat oven to 400°F. Total Cooking Time: 5 minutes. Bake at 400°F 4 minutes. Combo cook at 50% microwave power and 400°F 1 additional minute, or until lightly browned and cheese is soft. Let stand on baking sheet about 1 minute before serving.

Preheat oven to 350°F. Bake 8 to 10 minutes until lightly browned and cheese is soft. Let stand on baking sheet about 1 minute before serving.

Preheat oven to 450°F. Total Cooking Time: 5 minutes. Bake at 450°F 4 minutes. Combo cook at 50% microwave power and 450°F 1 additional minute, or until lightly browned and cheese is soft. Let stand on baking sheet about 1 minute before serving.

Preheat oven to 400°F. Bake 8 minutes, or until lightly browned and cheese is soft. Let stand on baking sheet about 1 minute before serving.

Cook at 75% microwave power 4 minutes, or until cheese is soft and coating is set. Let stand on baking sheet about 1 minute before serving.

* In microwave method, be sure to use a microwave safe baking dish.

Cheese Triangles ———————— 36 appetizers

1 cup ricotta or crumbled feta cheese
1/4 cup grated Romano cheese
2 tablespoons chopped fresh dill
1 egg, lightly beaten
1 egg yolk, lightly beaten
1/4 teaspoon freshly ground pepper
9 sheets phyllo dough (about 1/4 pound), thawed
1/4 cup butter or margarine, melted

Combine cheeses, dill, egg, egg yolk, and pepper; set aside. Working quickly, cut phyllo dough into strips measuring about 3×15 inches. Place on damp towel and cover with another damp towel. Remove strips, one at a time, from under towel. Brush strip with some of the butter and place about 1/2 tablespoon cheese mixture on one end. Fold strip over filling, making a triangle. Continue to fold, keeping edges straight, to end of strip forming a triangle. Repeat with remaining strips and filling. Brush triangles with remaining butter. Place about half the triangles on large baking sheet.

Preheat oven to 400°F. Total Cooking Time: 8 minutes. Combo cook at 50% microwave power and 400°F 3 minutes. Bake at 400°F 5 additional minutes, or until lightly browned. Repeat with remaining triangles.

Preheat oven to 375°F. Bake 15 to 20 minutes until lightly browned, rotating once. Repeat with remaining triangles.

Preheat oven to 450°F. Total Cooking Time: 8 minutes. Combo cook at 50% microwave power and 450°F 3 minutes. Bake at 450°F 5 additional minutes, or until lightly browned. Repeat with remaining triangles.

Preheat oven to 425°F. Bake 15 to 20 minutes until lightly browned. Repeat with remaining triangles.

Not recommended.

Cheese-Mushroom Roll-Ups _ 24 appetizers

½ pound mushrooms, minced
1 tablespoon butter or
    margarine
¼ teaspoon fines herbes or
    thyme
¼ teaspoon salt
2 tablespoons cornstarch
2 tablespoons dry white
    wine
1½ ounces cream cheese (half
    of 3-ounce package)
1 sheet frozen puff pastry
    (half of 17½-ounce package),
    thawed
1 egg yolk, beaten

Combine mushrooms, butter, fines herbes, and salt in 2-quart microwave safe casserole. Cook at 100% microwave power 5 minutes, or until very tender, stirring once. Blend cornstarch and wine. Stir into mushroom mixture. Cook at 100% microwave power 4 minutes, or until thickened, stirring once. Cut cream cheese into chunks and stir into mushroom mixture until smooth. Chill mixture well. Place cold puff pastry on lightly floured surface. Cut pastry in half lengthwise. Spread chilled mushroom mixture on each piece of pastry to within ¼ inch of one long edge. Brush edge with some of the egg yolk. Roll up starting from opposite long edge. Press seam to seal. Place rolled pastry on plate and freeze 20 minutes, or until firm. Brush rolls with remaining egg yolk; cut each roll into 12 pieces. Place rolls, cut-side down, on lightly greased baking sheet.

 Preheat oven to 325°F. Total Cooking Time: 13 to 15 minutes. Combo cook at 50% microwave power and 325°F 3 minutes. Bake at 325°F 10 to 12 additional minutes until lightly browned and flaky. Cool slightly before removing from baking sheet.

 Preheat oven to 300°F. Bake 18 to 20 minutes until lightly browned and flaky, rotating once. Cool slightly before removing from baking sheet.

 Preheat oven to 375°F. Total Cooking Time: 13 to 15 minutes. Combo cook at 50% microwave power and 375°F 3 minutes. Bake at 375°F 10 to 12 additional minutes until lightly browned and flaky. Cool slightly before removing from baking sheet.

 Preheat oven to 350°F. Bake 18 to 20 minutes until lightly browned and flaky. Cool slightly before removing from baking sheet.

 Not recommended.

Chicken Wing Appetizers ———— 20 servings

½ cup soy sauce
⅓ cup dry sherry
1 tablespoon minced candied
    ginger
2 pounds chicken wings
1 egg white
1 cup dry bread crumbs

Combine soy sauce, sherry, and ginger in plastic bag. Cut chicken wings apart at joints and discard wing tips. Place remaining wing sections in bag with marinade. Close bag tightly, pressing out as much air as possible. Shake bag to coat chicken with marinade. Refrigerate at least 2 hours or overnight, turning occasionally. Remove wings from marinade. Beat egg white and 1 tablespoon water. Dip wings in egg, then in bread crumbs. Place on lightly greased baking sheet.*

 Preheat oven to 375°F. Combo cook at 50% microwave power and 375°F 15 minutes, or until browned and crisp.

 Preheat oven to 350°F. Bake 25 to 30 minutes until browned and crisp, rotating once.

 Preheat oven to 425°F. Combo cook at 50% microwave power and 425°F 15 minutes, or until browned and crisp.

 Preheat oven to 400°F. Bake 25 to 30 minutes until browned and crisp.

 Cook at 100% microwave power 8 to 9 minutes until tender.

*In microwave method, be sure to use a glass baking dish.

Spiced Spareribs _____ 12 servings

½ cup plum preserves
¼ cup soy sauce
2 tablespoons dry sherry
2 teaspoons ground ginger
1 clove garlic, minced
2 pounds spareribs, cut
    into 1-rib portions

Place preserves in small glass bowl. Cook at 100% microwave power 1 to 2 minutes until melted and smooth. Stir in soy sauce, sherry, ginger, and garlic. Add spareribs. Cover and refrigerate at least 1 hour or overnight, turning occasionally.

 Place rack in 4th position from bottom. Preheat broiler 3 minutes. Arrange spareribs on rack set over broiler pan. Combo cook at 75% microwave power and broil 10 minutes, or until well browned and tender.

 Place rack in 4th position from bottom. Preheat oven to 400°F 3 minutes. Arrange spareribs on rack set over broiler pan. Broil 45 to 50 minutes until well browned and tender, brushing occasionally with sauce and rotating once.

 Place rack in 4th position from bottom. Preheat broiler 3 minutes. Arrange spareribs on broiler pan. Combo cook at 75% microwave power and broil 10 minutes. Turn spareribs and broil 3 to 5 minutes until well browned and tender.

 Preheat broiler 3 minutes. Place rack in 2nd position from bottom. Arrange spareribs on broiler pan. Broil 50 to 60 minutes until well browned and tender, turning often and brushing occasionally with sauce.

 Place spareribs in large glass baking dish. Brush with sauce. Cook at 100% microwave power 8 minutes. Drain liquid. Cook at 75% microwave power 23 to 25 minutes until tender and glazed, brushing with sauce twice.

Stuffed Clams ‹———————————————›

12 large clams
¾ cup spaghetti sauce
½ teaspoon oregano
   (optional)
1 clove garlic, minced
   (optional)
¾ cup fresh bread crumbs
3 tablespoons chopped fresh
   parsley
2 tablespoons grated
   Parmesan cheese

Scrub clams with stiff brush. Place in water to cover and soak 15 minutes. Place in large glass baking dish. Cover and cook at 100% microwave power 6 to 8 minutes just until shells open. Remove clams that have opened and microwave unopened clams a few minutes longer. Discard juice and any clams that do not open. Cool clams slightly; twist off top shell and discard. Remove clams from bottom shells and chop coarsely. Combine with spaghetti sauce, oregano, and garlic. Spoon mixture into shells. Return stuffed clams to baking dish.

 Combine bread crumbs, parsley, and cheese; sprinkle over clam mixture. Preheat oven to 350°F. Combo cook at 50% microwave power and 350°F 7 minutes, or until hot and lightly browned.

 Combine bread crumbs, parsley, and cheese; sprinkle over clam mixture. Preheat oven to 300°F. Bake 15 minutes, or until hot and lightly browned.

 Combine bread crumbs, parsley, and cheese; sprinkle over clam mixture. Preheat oven to 400°F. Combo cook at 50% microwave power and 400°F 7 minutes, or until hot and lightly browned.

 Combine bread crumbs, parsley, and cheese; sprinkle over clam mixture. Preheat oven to 350°F. Bake 15 to 20 minutes until hot and lightly browned.

 Toast bread crumbs in skillet over moderate heat. Combine with parsley and cheese; set aside. Cook filled clam shells at 100% microwave power 3 to 4 minutes until hot and bubbly. Sprinkle with bread crumb mixture and cook at 100% microwave power 1 minute, or until topping is hot.

Swedish Meatballs _____ 8 servings

1 pound lean ground beef
½ cup dry bread crumbs
1 cup heavy cream, divided
¼ cup dry sherry
¼ teaspoon nutmeg
¼ teaspoon salt
¼ cup all-purpose flour
½ cup condensed consommé,
   undiluted
Paprika

Combine beef, bread crumbs, ½ cup cream, sherry, nutmeg, and salt. Shape into 1-inch balls and coat with flour. Place in 1½-quart casserole.* Combine remaining ½ cup cream and consommé. Pour over meatballs.

MICROWAVE FIRST

Preheat oven to 300°F. Total Cooking Time: 25 minutes. Combo cook at 75% microwave power and 300°F 5 minutes. Bake at 300°F 20 additional minutes, or until meatballs are tender and sauce is thickened. Stir gently and sprinkle with paprika before serving.

Cover and bake at 300°F 50 to 55 minutes until meatballs are tender and sauce is thickened. Stir gently and sprinkle with paprika before serving.

MICROWAVE FIRST

Preheat oven to 350°F. Total Cooking Time: 25 minutes. Combo cook at 75% microwave power and 350°F 5 minutes. Bake at 350°F 20 additional minutes, or until meatballs are tender and sauce is thickened. Stir gently and sprinkle with paprika before serving.

Cover and bake at 350°F 50 to 55 minutes until meatballs are tender and sauce is thickened. Stir gently and sprinkle with paprika before serving.

Cook at 75% microwave power 8 to 9 minutes until meatballs are tender and sauce is thickened. Stir gently and sprinkle with paprika before serving.

* In microwave method, be sure to use a microwave safe casserole.

Coquille St. Jacques ——————— 8 servings

1 pound bay scallops
¼ pound mushrooms, sliced
¼ cup dry white wine
1 clove garlic, minced
½ teaspoon salt
1 tablespoon lemon juice
2 teaspoons cornstarch
½ cup fresh bread crumbs
½ cup shredded Swiss cheese
2 tablespoons chopped fresh
parsley

Combine scallops, mushrooms, wine, garlic, and salt in 2-quart microwave safe casserole. Cook at 100% microwave power 6 minutes, stirring once. Remove scallops and mushrooms from broth with slotted spoon; set aside. Blend lemon juice and cornstarch. Stir into broth in casserole. Cook at 100% microwave power 6 minutes, stirring once. Spoon scallops and mushrooms into 8 scallop shells or ramekins and place on baking sheet.* Top with sauce.

Combine bread crumbs, cheese, and parsley. Sprinkle over sauce. Preheat oven to 375°F. Total Cooking Time: 8 minutes. Combo cook at 50% microwave power and 375°F 5 minutes. Bake at 375°F 3 additional minutes, or until lightly browned.

Combine bread crumbs, cheese, and parsley. Sprinkle over sauce. Preheat oven to 325°F. Bake 12 to 15 minutes until lightly browned.

Combine bread crumbs, cheese, and parsley. Sprinkle over sauce. Preheat oven to 425°F. Total Cooking Time: 8 minutes. Combo cook at 50% microwave power and 425°F 5 minutes. Bake at 425°F 3 additional minutes, or until lightly browned.

Combine bread crumbs, cheese, and parsley. Sprinkle over sauce. Preheat oven to 375°F. Bake 12 to 15 minutes until lightly browned.

Toast bread crumbs in skillet over moderate heat. Combine with cheese and parsley. Sprinkle over sauce. Cook at 100% microwave power 4 to 5 minutes until sauce is hot and cheese is melted.

* In microwave method, be sure to use microwave safe dishes.

Baba Ghanoush _____

1¼- pound eggplant
½ teaspoon salt
1 clove garlic, or to taste
3 teaspoons lemon juice
2 tablespoons olive oil
Fresh bread crumbs
(optional)
Sliced ripe olives
(optional)
Warm pita bread, cut
into wedges

Rinse eggplant and pat dry. Pierce in several places with sharp knife. Place in baking dish.* Cook as directed below. Cool until easy to handle. Cut in half and scoop out pulp. Place pulp in food processor or blender. Add salt, garlic, and lemon juice. Purée until smooth. Blend in oil until well mixed. If too thin, add 2 or 3 tablespoons bread crumbs and mix well. Spoon back into shell; garnish with olives. Serve as dip with pita bread.

 Combo cook at 75% microwave power and 350°F 12 to 13 minutes until very soft.

 Bake at 350°F 45 to 50 minutes until very soft.

 Combo cook at 75% microwave power and 400°F 12 to 13 minutes until very soft.

 Bake at 400°F 55 to 60 minutes until very soft.

 Cook at 100% microwave power 10 to 11 minutes until very soft.

* In microwave method, be sure to use a microwave safe baking dish.

Stuffed Artichokes ─────────── 6 appetizers

6 artichokes
1 can (7 ounces) tuna,
  drained
¾ cup chopped fresh parsley
2 tablespoons chopped
  capers
1 tablespoon lemon juice
2 egg whites
1 cup fresh bread crumbs
  Hollandaise sauce or
  melted butter

Trim stems of artichokes even with bottom. Cut off 1 inch from top and trim tip of each leaf with scissors. Rinse and place in microwave safe casserole. Add ¼ cup water. Cover and cook at 100% microwave power 10 minutes, or until a leaf can be pulled from artichoke easily. Cool until easy to handle. Pull leaves apart in center of each artichoke and pull out tiny yellow and purple leaves in center. Scrape out fuzzy "choke" with spoon. Rinse and invert to drain. Flake tuna and combine with parsley, capers, and lemon juice. Beat egg whites until stiff peaks form. Fold into tuna mixture. Fold in bread crumbs. Spoon mixture into artichokes. Return to casserole.

Preheat oven to 350°F. Total Cooking Time: 10 minutes. Combo cook at 75% microwave power and 350°F 5 minutes. Bake at 350°F 5 additional minutes, or until filling is hot and lightly browned. Serve with Hollandaise sauce or melted butter.

Preheat oven to 325°F. Bake 20 minutes, or until filling is hot and lightly browned. Serve with Hollandaise sauce or melted butter.

Preheat oven to 400°F. Total Cooking Time: 10 minutes. Combo cook at 75% microwave power and 400°F 5 minutes. Bake at 400°F 5 additional minutes, or until filling is hot and lightly browned. Serve with Hollandaise sauce or melted butter.

Preheat oven to 375°F. Bake 20 minutes, or until filling is hot and lightly browned. Serve with Hollandaise sauce or melted butter.

Cook at 100% microwave power 8 to 9 minutes until filling is hot. Let stand 5 minutes before serving. Serve with Hollandaise sauce or melted butter.

Country Pâté

1 pound ground pork
1 pound ground veal
1 onion, minced
½ cup dry white wine
2 tablespoons brandy
2 teaspoons salt
½ teaspoon thyme
½ teaspoon allspice
½ teaspoon freshly ground
    pepper
¼ teaspoon nutmeg
2 cloves garlic, minced
    Radishes, carrots, and
        chives (optional)
    Crackers

Combine all ingredients except radishes, carrots, chives, and crackers in large bowl. Mix until smooth. Pack into greased 5½-cup fluted baking dish or 8×4-inch loaf pan.* Cook as directed below. Cover and chill several hours. To serve, invert pâté onto serving plate. Gently scrape off fat and jelled broth. Discard fat. Heat broth and spoon over pâté to glaze. Cut radish flowers or carrot curls and arrange on pâté. Use chives for stems and leaves. Surround with radish flowers or carrot curls. Serve with crackers.

 Combo cook at 50% microwave power and 300°F 30 minutes, or until firm and slightly brown.

 Bake at 275°F 2 hours, or until firm.

 Combo cook at 50% microwave power and 350°F 30 minutes, or until firm and slightly brown.

 Bake at 325°F 2 hours, or until firm.

 Cover with waxed paper. Cook at 50% microwave power 35 to 38 minutes until firm.

* In microwave method, be sure to use a microwave safe baking dish or loaf pan.

The Main Course

Meat Roasting Guide

- Roast meat on rack in shallow roasting pan.
- Remove meat from oven and cover lightly with a tent of folded foil. Let stand 10 to 15 minutes before carving.
- Meat internal temperature will rise 5°F to 10°F during stand time.
- Check meat internal temperature with meat thermometer inserted in thickest part of meat or in joint of poultry. Be sure tip does not touch bone or rest in fat.
- Cover thin pieces of meat and bone tips with small pieces of foil to prevent burning.
- When using a meat thermometer during cooking, be sure to use the correct type for the cooking method.
  For combination cooking, use only Caloric's Cook 'n Roast Thermometer, which is safe for microwave and heat cookery.
  For electric radiant or gas convection roasting, a conventional meat roasting thermometer may be used. For microwave cookery, use either Caloric's Cook 'n Roast thermometer or other thin stemmed microwave safe thermometer.

CUT OF MEAT & WEIGHT	Internal Temp. (F°) On Removal From Oven	Oven Temp. (F°)	% Microwave Power	Minutes/Pound	Oven Temp. (F°)	Minutes/Pound	Oven Temp. (F°)	% Microwave Power	Minutes/Pound	Oven Temp. (F°)	Minutes/Pound	% Microwave Power	Minutes/Pound
BEEF													
Beef Rib Roast 6-8 lb.													
rare	130	300	50	9-10	275	23	350	50	9-10	325	23	75	8-9
med	145	300	50	11-12	275	27	350	50	10-12	325	27	75	9-10
well	165	300	50	13-14	275	30-32	350	50	11-14	325	30-32	75	11
Beef Rib Roast 4-6 lb.													
rare	130	300	50	8-10	275	25-28	350	50	8-10	325	25-28	75	7½-8
med	145	300	50	9-11	275	33-35	350	50	9-11	325	33-35	75	8-9
well	165	300	50	11-14	275	40	350	50	11-14	325	40	75	10-11

CUT OF MEAT & WEIGHT	Internal Temp. (F°) On Removal From Oven	Oven Temp. (F°)	% Microwave Power	Minutes / Pound	Oven Temp. (F°)	Minutes / Pound	Oven Temp. (F°)	% Microwave Power	Minutes / Pound	Oven Temp. (F°)	Minutes / Pound	% Microwave Power	Minutes / Pound
Beef Boneless Rolled Rib 5-7 lb. — rare	130	300	50	9-11	275	30	350	50	9-10	325	30	75	8-9
med	145	300	50	10-12	275	35	350	50	10-12	325	35	75	9-10
well	165	300	50	11-14	275	40-45	350	50	11-14	325	40-45	75	11-12
Beef Rib Eye 4-6 lb. — rare	130	300	50	10	275	18	350	50	10	325	18	75	8
med	145	300	50	12	275	20	350	50	12	325	20	75	9
well	165	300	50	13-14	275	22	350	50	13-14	325	22	75	11
Beef Tenderloin (whole) 4-6 lb. — rare	130	400	50	6	375	40-55 min. total	450	50	6	425	40-55 min. total	75	6-7
med	145	400	50	7	375	55-65 min. total	450	50	7	425	55-65 min. total	75	8-9
Beef Tenderloin (half) 2-3 lb. — rare	130	400	50	7	375	35-45 min. total	450	50	7	425	35-45 min. total	75	7-8
med	145	400	50	8	375	40-50 min total	450	50	8	425	40-50 min. total	75	8-9
Boneless Beef Rump 4-6 lb.	130-160	300	50	15-17	275	23-28	350	50	15-17	325	23-28	50	18
Sirloin Tip 4 lb.	130-160	300	50	18-22	275	33-38	350	50	18-22	325	33-38	50	20-23
VEAL													
Veal Leg 5-8 lb.	160-170	300	50	12-14	275	30	350	50	12-14	325	30	50	13-15
Veal Loin 4-6 lb.	160-170	300	50	12-14	275	30-33	350	50	12-14	325	30-33	50	13-15

THE MAIN COURSE

CUT OF MEAT & WEIGHT	Internal Temp. (F°) On Removal From Oven	Oven Temp. (F°)	% Microwave Power	Minutes / Pound	Oven Temp. (F°)	Minutes / Pound	Oven Temp. (F°)	% Microwave Power	Minutes / Pound	Oven Temp. (F°)	Minutes / Pound	% Microwave Power	Minutes / Pound
Veal Rib 3-5 lb.	160-170	300	50	12-14	275	35	350	50	12-14	325	35	50	14-16
Boneless Veal Shoulder	160-170	300	50	15-16	275	40-45	350	50	15-16	325	40-45	50	17-19
FRESH PORK													
Pork Loin center 3-5 lb.	170	300	50	11-12	275	30-35	350	50	11-12	325	30-35	75	14-16
half 5-7 lb.	170	170	50	11-13	275	35-40	350	50	11-13	325	35-40	75	12-14
Pork Picnic Shoulder 5-8 lb.	170	300	50	12-14	275	35	350	50	12-14	325	35	75	13-14
Boneless Arm Picnic 3-5 lb.	170	300	50	15-16	275	40	350	50	15-16	325	40	75	14-17
Pork Leg (Fresh Ham) 12-16 lb.	170	300	50	10-12	275	25	350	50	10-12	325	25	75	11-13
half 5-8 lb.	170	300	50	11-14	275	30-40	350	50	11-14	325	30-40	75	12-14
SMOKED PORK													
Ham whole 10-14 lb.	160	300	50	11-13	275	18-20	350	50	11-13	325	18-20	75	10-12
half 5-7 lb.	160	300	50	12-14	275	22-25	350	50	12-14	325	22-25	75	11-13
Smoked Arm Picnic Shoulder 5-8 lb.	170	300	50	12-14	275	35	350	50	12-14	325	35	75	13-15
Ham (Fully Cooked) whole 10-13 lb.	140	300	50	7-9	275	15	350	50	7-9	325	15	75	8-9
half 5-7 lb.	140	300	50	8-10	275	20	350	50	8-10	325	20	75	10

CUT OF MEAT & WEIGHT	Internal Temp. (F°) On Removal From Oven	Oven Temp. (F°)	% Microwave Power	Minutes/Pound	Oven Temp. (F°)	Minutes/Pound	Oven Temp. (F°)	% Microwave Power	Minutes/Pound	Oven Temp. (F°)	Minutes/Pound	% Microwave Power	Minutes/Pound
LAMB													
Leg 5-8 lb. rare / well	140-150 / 160	300 / 300	50 / 50	8-10 / 10-12	275 / 275	24 / 30	350 / 350	50 / 50	8-10 / 10-12	325 / 325	24 / 30	75 / 75	7-10 / 10-12
Lamb Shoulder (bone-in) 4-6 lb. rare / well	140-150 / 160	300 / 300	50 / 50	9-11 / 11-13	275 / 275	25-27 / 30	350 / 350	50 / 50	9-11 / 11-13	325 / 325	25-27 / 30	75 / 75	8-10 / 10-12
Lamb Shoulder (boneless) 3-5 lb. rare / well	140-150 / 160	350	50	10-12 / 12-14	275	33-35 / 40	350	50	10-12 / 12-14	325	33-35 / 40	75	9-12 / 11-14
Lamb Shoulder Cushion 3-5 lb. rare / well	140-150 / 160	350	50	10-13 / 12-14	275	25 / 30	350	50	10-13 / 12-14	325	25 / 30	75	9-12 / 11-14
POULTRY													
Turkey (Stuffed) 8-12 lb.	180	300	75	1-1¼ hours total	275	4-5 hours total	350	75	1-1¼ hours total	325	4-5 hours total	75	1¼-1½ hours total
12-16 lb.	180	300	75	1-1¼ hours total	275	4½-5½ hours total	350	75	1¼-1¾ hours total	325	4½-5½ hours total	75	1½-2 hours total
16-20 lb.	180	300	75	1¾-2¼ hours total	275	5½-6½ hours total	350	75	1¾-2¼ hours total	325	5½-6½ hours total	75	2-2¼ hours total
20-24 lb.	180	300	75	2-2¾ hours total	275	6-7½ hours total	325	75	2-2¾ hours total	325	6-7½ hours total	75	2-3 hours total

CUT OF MEAT & WEIGHT	Internal Temp. (F°) On Removal From Oven	Oven Temp. (F°)	% Microwave Power	Minutes / Pound	Oven Temp. (F°)	Minutes / Pound	Oven Temp. (F°)	% Microwave Power	Minutes / Pound	Oven Temp. (F°)	Minutes / Pound	% Microwave Power	Minutes / Pound
Turkey (Unstuffed) 8-12 lb.	180-185	300	75	40-60 min total	275	3-4 hours total	350	75	40-60 min total	325	3-4 hours total	75	40-60 min total
12-16 lb.	180-185	300	75	45-75 min total	275	4-5 hours total	350	75	45-75 min total	325	4-5 hours total	75	55-80 min total
16-20 lb.	180-185	300	75	1-1½ hours total	275	4½-6 hours total	350	75	1-1½ hours total	325	4½-6 hours total	75	1¼-1½ hours total
20-24 lb.	180-185	300	75	1½-2 hours total	275	5½-6½ hours total	350	75	1½-2 hours total	325	5½-6½ hours total	75	1½-2 hours total
Roasting Chicken (Stuffed) 4-6 lb.	180-185	325	50	8-10	300	2½-3½ hours total	375	50	8-10	350	2½-3½ hours total	50	9-10
Roasting Chicken (Unstuffed) 4-6 lb.	180-185	325	50	7-9	300	2-3 hours total	375	50	7-9	350	2-3 hours total	75	5-7
Broiler Fryer (Stuffed) 2½-4 lb.	180-185	325	50	9-10	325	2-2½ hours total	375	50	9-10	375	2-2½ hours total	75	6-7
Broiler Fryer (Unstuffed) 2½-4 lb.	180-185	325	50	7-9	325	1½-2 hours total	375	50	7-9	375	1½-2 hours total	75	4-7
Duckling* 4-5 lb.	190	325	50	9-12	300	2½-3 hours total	375	50	9-12	350	2½-3 hours total	75	10-12

*Pierce skin in many places with fork.

CUT OF MEAT & WEIGHT	Internal Temp. (F°) On Removal From Oven	Oven Temp. (F°)	% Microwave Power	Minutes / Pound	Oven Temp. (F°)	Minutes / Pound	Oven Temp. (F°)	% Microwave Power	Minutes / Pound	Oven Temp. (F°)	Minutes / Pound	% Microwave Power	Minutes / Pound
Goose* (Stuffed) 6-8 lb.	190	325	50	10-12	300	3-3½ hours total	375	50	10-12	350	3-3½ hours total	75	8
8-12 lb.	190	325	50	9-11	300	3½-4½ hours total	375	50	9-11	350	3½-4½ hours total	75	7
Goose* (Unstuffed) 6-8 lb.	190	325	50	9-11	300	2½-3 hours total	375	50	9-11	350	2½-3 hours total	75	6-8
8-12 lb.	190	325	50	7-10	300	3-4 hours total	375	50	7-10	350	3-4 hours total	75	5-6

* Pierce skin in many places with fork.

Hunan Shredded Beef _____ 4 to 6 servings

1 pound beef flank steak
1 cup beef broth
1/4 cup soy sauce
1 onion, cut into thin
   slivers
1/8 teaspoon cayenne
2 tablespoons cornstarch
1/2 pound carrots, cut into
   julienne strips
1 package (6 ounces) frozen
   pea pods, thawed
1/4 pound mushrooms, sliced
1 red pepper, cut into
   thin strips

Cut beef lengthwise into thin slices. Cut slices in half and place in 2½-quart casserole.* Add beef broth, soy sauce, onion, cayenne, and ½ cup water. Cover casserole. Combine cornstarch and 3 tablespoons water; set aside.

 Combo cook at 100% microwave power and 275°F 10 minutes. Reduce microwave power and combo cook at 75% microwave power and 275°F 25 minutes, or until tender. Blend in cornstarch mixture. Add vegetables and stir to coat. Cover and combo cook at 100% microwave power and 275°F 7 to 8 minutes until vegetables are desired tenderness. Serve over hot cooked rice, if desired.

 Bake at 275°F 1 hour 15 minutes, or until tender. Blend in cornstarch mixture. Add vegetables and stir to coat. Cover and bake 20 to 30 minutes until vegetables are desired tenderness. Serve over hot cooked rice, if desired.

 Combo cook at 100% microwave power and 325°F 10 minutes. Reduce microwave power and combo cook at 75% microwave power and 325°F 25 minutes, or until tender. Blend in cornstarch mixture. Add vegetables and stir to coat. Cover and combo cook at 100% microwave power and 325°F 7 to 8 minutes until vegetables are desired tenderness. Serve over hot cooked rice, if desired.

 Bake at 325°F 1 hour 15 minutes, or until meat is tender. Blend in cornstarch mixture. Add vegetables and stir to coat. Cover and bake 20 to 30 minutes until vegetables are of desired tenderness. Serve over hot cooked rice, if desired.

 Cook at 100% microwave power 10 minutes. Reduce power and cook at 75% microwave power 30 minutes, or until tender. Blend in cornstarch mixture. Add vegetables and stir to coat. Cook at 100% microwave power 7 to 8 minutes until vegetables are desired tenderness. Serve over hot cooked rice, if desired.

* In microwave method, be sure to use a microwave safe casserole.

Meatloaf _____ 8 servings

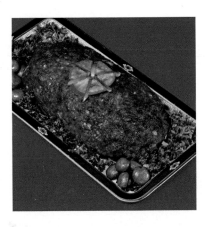

2 pounds lean ground beef
2 cups fresh bread crumbs
1 onion, minced
¼ cup minced celery
½ cup tomato juice
2 eggs, lightly beaten
1 tablespoon Worcestershire
 sauce
1½ teaspoons salt
 Few drops hot pepper sauce
 Tomato, green pepper, and
 mushrooms (optional)

Crumble beef into large bowl. Add bread crumbs, onion, and celery. Mix lightly. Blend tomato juice, eggs, Worcestershire, salt, and hot pepper sauce in small bowl. Add to beef mixture and stir until well combined. Place beef in 9×13-inch baking dish* and pat into an oval loaf.

 Combo cook at 75% microwave power and 350°F 25 minutes, or until lightly browned. Let stand 5 minutes before slicing. Garnish with tomato, green pepper, and mushrooms.

 Bake at 300°F 1 hour 15 minutes, or until lightly browned, rotating once. Let stand 5 minutes before slicing. Garnish with tomato, green pepper, and mushrooms.

 Combo cook at 75% microwave power and 400°F 25 minutes, or until lightly browned. Let stand 5 minutes before slicing. Garnish with tomato, green pepper, and mushrooms.

 Bake at 350°F 1 hour 15 minutes, or until lightly browned. Let stand 5 minutes before slicing. Garnish with tomato, green pepper, and mushrooms.

 Cook at 75% microwave power 28 to 30 minutes until juices are clear and lightly browned. Let stand 5 minutes before slicing. Garnish with tomato, green pepper, and mushrooms.

* In microwave method, be sure to use a microwave safe baking dish.

New England Boiled Dinner 8 servings

3½- to 4-pound corned beef
     brisket
1 bay leaf
6 whole allspice
6 whole cloves
1 clove garlic
½ teaspoon peppercorns
1 cinnamon stick
1 pound carrots, peeled and
     cut into chunks
1 pound green beans
1 pint Brussels sprouts
     (optional)
10 small white onions

Place corned beef and 4 cups water in 4-quart casserole.* Tie bay leaf, allspice, cloves, garlic, peppercorns, and cinnamon stick in cheesecloth; add to casserole. Cover casserole.

 Combo cook at 100% microwave power and 275°F 15 minutes. Reduce microwave power and combo cook at 50% microwave power and 275°F 30 minutes. Add vegetables, cover, and combo cook at 50% microwave power and 275°F 25 to 30 minutes until beef and vegetables are tender. Remove beef from casserole and slice. Surround with vegetables and serve.

 Bake at 275°F 2 hours 30 minutes. Add vegetables, cover, and bake 1 hour, or until beef and vegetables are tender. Check occasionally and add a little more hot water, if needed. Remove beef from casserole and slice. Surround with vegetables and serve.

 Combo cook at 100% microwave power and 325°F 15 minutes. Reduce microwave power and combo cook at 50% microwave power and 325°F 30 minutes. Add vegetables, cover, and combo cook at 50% microwave power and 325°F 25 to 30 minutes until beef and vegetables are tender. Remove beef from casserole and slice. Surround with vegetables and serve.

 Bake at 325°F 2 hours 30 minutes. Add vegetables, cover, and bake 1 hour, or until beef and vegetables are tender. Check occasionally and add a little more hot water, if needed. Remove beef from casserole and slice. Surround with vegetables and serve.

 Cook beef at 100% microwave power 15 minutes. Reduce power and cook at 50% microwave power 40 minutes. Add vegetables, cover, and cook at 50% microwave power 30 to 35 minutes until beef and vegetables are tender. Remove beef from casserole and slice. Surround with vegetables and serve.

* In microwave method, be sure to use a microwave safe casserole.

Sauerbraten ————————————

4- pound beef chuck cross rib
   pot roast, boneless
3 onions, sliced
2 cups dry red wine
½ cup vinegar
2 tablespoons mixed whole
   pickling spice
2 tablespoons all-purpose
   flour
2 tablespoons vegetable oil
½ cup gingersnap cookie
   crumbs
½ cup dairy sour cream
   (optional)
  Salt and freshly ground
   pepper, to taste
  Hot cooked noodles
   (optional)

Place beef in 4-quart glass casserole. Add onions. Combine wine, vinegar, and pickling spice. Pour over beef and onions. Cover and refrigerate 1 to 3 days, turning beef occasionally. Remove beef from marinade and pat dry with paper towels. Coat with flour and brown in hot oil in skillet. Return beef to casserole. Cover and cook as directed below. Remove beef from cooking liquid and keep warm. Stir cookie crumbs into liquid and cook at 100% microwave power 3 to 5 minutes until gravy is slightly thickened. Strain gravy into large bowl; blend in sour cream. Sprinkle with salt and pepper. Slice beef and serve with gravy and noodles.

 Combo cook at 100% microwave power and 300°F 15 minutes. Reduce microwave power and combo cook at 50% microwave power and 300°F 1 hour, or until tender.

 Bake at 275°F 2½ hours to 3 hours until tender. Check occasionally and add a little more wine or water, if needed.

 Combo cook at 100% microwave power and 350°F 15 minutes. Reduce microwave power and combo cook at 50% microwave power and 350°F 1 hour, or until tender.

 Bake at 325°F 2½ hours to 3 hours, or until tender. Check occasionally and add a little more wine or water, if needed.

 Cook at 100% microwave power 20 minutes. Reduce power and cook at 75% microwave power 50 to 60 minutes until tender.

Beef Rolls _____ 6 servings

1½ pounds beef round steak,
    cut about ¼-inch thick
⅓ cup all-purpose flour
1 teaspoon salt
¼ teaspoon freshly ground
    pepper
1 cup shredded carrots
2 tablespoons vegetable oil
2 leeks or 1 onion, finely
    chopped
½ pound mushrooms, sliced
½ cup dry red wine
½ cup beef broth
1 bay leaf

Cut beef into 6 pieces. Combine flour, salt, and pepper. Coat beef with flour mixture. Pound beef until very thin, dusting with flour mixture to prevent sticking. Sprinkle carrots over beef; roll up. Tie with string or secure with wooden toothpicks. Brown rolls lightly in hot oil in skillet. Remove rolls; place in 2-quart casserole.* Sauté leeks and mushrooms in skillet until lightly browned. Add 1 cup water and stir to loosen browned bits. Pour over beef rolls in casserole. Add wine, beef broth, and bay leaf. Cover casserole.

 Combo cook at 100% microwave power and 275°F 10 minutes. Reduce microwave power and combo cook at 50% microwave power and 275°F 40 minutes, or until tender. Discard bay leaf and serve with cooking liquid spooned over rolls.

 Bake at 250°F 2 hours, or until tender. Check occasionally and add a little more liquid, if needed. Discard bay leaf and serve with cooking liquid spooned over rolls.

 Combo cook at 100% microwave power and 325°F 10 minutes. Reduce microwave power and combo cook at 50% microwave power and 325°F 40 minutes, or until tender. Discard bay leaf and serve with cooking liquid spooned over rolls.

 Bake at 300°F 2 hours, or until tender. Check occasionally and add a little more liquid, if needed. Discard bay leaf and serve with cooking liquid spooned over rolls.

 Cook at 100% microwave power 10 minutes. Reduce power and cook at 50% microwave power 45 minutes, or until tender. Discard bay leaf and serve with cooking liquid spooned over rolls.

* In microwave method, be sure to use a microwave safe casserole.

Pot Roast _____ 6 to 8 servings

2½ pounds beef chuck steak
(about 1½ inches thick)
2 tablespoons vegetable oil
1 cup chopped carrots
1 cup chopped onions
½ cup chopped celery
1 clove garlic, minced
2 cups beef broth
6 to 8 new potatoes
1 pound green beans
2 onions, quartered and
separated into layers

Brown beef in hot oil in large flameproof casserole.* Remove beef and set aside. Add carrots, chopped onions, celery, and garlic to casserole; sauté until tender. Stir in beef broth and 1 cup water. Add beef and heat to boiling. Cover casserole.

 Combo cook at 100% microwave power and 275°F 10 minutes. Reduce microwave power and combo cook at 75% microwave power and 275°F 25 minutes. Turn beef over. Add potatoes, beans, and quartered onions. Cover and combo cook at 75% microwave power and 275°F 20 to 25 minutes until beef and vegetables are tender.

 Bake at 275°F 1 hour 30 minutes. Add potatoes, beans, and quartered onions. Add a little hot water, if needed. Cover and bake 1 hour, or until beef and vegetables are tender.

 Combo cook at 100% microwave power and 325°F 10 minutes. Reduce microwave power and combo cook at 75% microwave power and 325°F 25 minutes. Turn beef over. Add potatoes, beans, and quartered onions. Cover and combo cook at 75% microwave power and 325°F 20 to 25 minutes until beef and vegetables are tender.

 Bake at 325°F 1 hour 30 minutes. Add potatoes, beans, and quartered onions. Add a little hot water, if needed. Cover and bake 1 hour, or until beef and vegetables are tender.

 Cook at 100% microwave power 10 minutes. Reduce power and cook at 75% microwave power 30 minutes. Turn beef over. Add potatoes, beans, and quartered onions. Cover and cook at 75% microwave power 25 to 30 minutes until beef and vegetables are tender.

* In microwave method, be sure casserole is microwave safe as well as flameproof.

Swiss Steak _____

2 pounds beef round steak
1/4 cup all-purpose flour
1 1/2 teaspoons salt
1/4 teaspoon freshly ground
  pepper
1/2 teaspoon thyme
2 tablespoons vegetable oil
2 onions, sliced
1 green pepper, seeded and
  sliced
1 can (16 ounces) tomatoes,
  cut up, liquid reserved

Cut beef into 8 pieces. Combine flour, salt, pepper, and thyme. Coat beef with flour mixture. Heat oil in skillet. Brown beef lightly on both sides and place in shallow 2 1/2-quart casserole.* Sprinkle remaining flour mixture over beef. Add onions, green pepper, tomatoes with liquid, and 1/2 cup water. Cover casserole.

 Combo cook at 50% microwave power and 275°F 40 to 45 minutes until beef is tender.

 Bake at 275°F 2 hours, or until beef is tender.

 Combo cook at 50% microwave power and 325°F 40 to 45 minutes until beef is tender.

 Bake at 325°F 2 hours, or until beef is tender.

 Cook at 50% microwave power 45 to 50 minutes until beef is tender.

*In microwave method, be sure to use a microwave safe casserole.

Deviled Beef Short Ribs

4 pounds beef short ribs
2 tablespoons vegetable oil
2 onions, sliced
1/4 cup prepared mustard
1/4 cup thick steak sauce
1/4 cup firmly packed brown
    sugar
1 tablespoon horseradish
1 teaspoon salt
1 clove garlic, minced

Brown ribs in hot oil in large flameproof casserole.* Remove ribs as they brown. Sauté onions in drippings in casserole. Add 1 cup water and stir to loosen browned bits. Stir in mustard, steak sauce, brown sugar, horseradish, salt, and garlic; heat to boiling. Add ribs; turn to coat with sauce. Cover casserole.

 Combo cook at 50% microwave power and 275°F 45 to 50 minutes until tender.

 Bake at 275°F 2 to 2½ hours until tender. Check occasionally and add a little more liquid, if needed.

 Combo cook at 50% microwave power and 325°F 45 to 50 minutes until tender.

 Bake at 325°F 2 to 2½ hours until tender. Check occasionally and add a little more liquid, if needed.

 Cook at 50% microwave power 50 to 55 minutes until tender.

* In microwave method, be sure casserole is microwave safe as well as flameproof.

Browned Beef Stew _____ 6 to 8 servings

⅓ cup all-purpose flour
1 teaspoon oregano
1 teaspoon thyme
1½ teaspoons salt
½ teaspoon freshly ground
    pepper
2 pounds beef for stew, cut
    into 1-inch cubes
¼ cup vegetable oil
2 onions, sliced
1 can (12 ounces) beer
1 pound carrots, peeled and
    cut into 1-inch pieces
½ pound small mushrooms
1 pound zucchini, cut into
    1-inch pieces

Combine flour, oregano, thyme, salt, and pepper. Use to coat meat. Brown meat in about half the oil, adding more as necessary. Place meat in 4-quart casserole*. Sprinkle any leftover flour mixture over meat. Sauté onions in skillet until lightly browned. Add 1 cup water to skillet and stir to loosen browned bits. Pour over meat in casserole. Add beer, carrots, and mushrooms to casserole. Cover.

 Combo cook at 100% microwave power and 275°F 10 minutes. Reduce microwave power and combo cook at 50% microwave power and 275°F 50 minutes, stirring once and adding a little hot water, if needed. Stir in zucchini, cover, and combo cook at 100% microwave power and 275°F 8 to 9 minutes until beef and vegetables are tender.

 Bake at 275°F 2 hours 30 minutes, or until beef is almost tender, stirring once and adding a little hot water, if needed. Stir in zucchini, cover, and bake 30 to 40 minutes until beef and vegetables are tender.

 Combo cook at 100% microwave power and 325°F 10 minutes. Reduce microwave power and combo cook at 50% microwave power and 325°F 50 minutes, stirring once and adding a little hot water, if needed. Stir in zucchini, cover, and combo cook at 100% microwave power and 325°F 8 to 9 minutes until beef and vegetables are tender.

 Bake at 325°F 2 hours 30 minutes, or until beef is almost tender, stirring once and adding a little hot water, if needed. Stir in zucchini, cover, and bake 30 to 40 minutes until beef and vegetables are tender.

 Cook at 100% microwave power 10 minutes. Reduce power and cook at 50% microwave power 1 hour, stirring once. Stir in zucchini, cover and cook at 100% microwave power 8 to 9 minutes until beef and vegetables are tender.

*In microwave method, be sure to use a microwave safe casserole.

Barbecued Spareribs _____ 4 to 6 servings

4 pounds spareribs
½ cup minced onion
2 cloves garlic, minced
¼ cup vegetable oil
1 can (8 ounces) tomato
    sauce
¼ cup firmly packed brown
    sugar
2 tablespoons vinegar
1 tablespoon chili powder
2 teaspoons salt
1 teaspoon dry mustard

Cut spareribs into 1-rib portions; set aside. Sauté onion and garlic in hot oil until onion is transparent. Stir in tomato sauce, brown sugar, vinegar, chili powder, salt, and mustard; heat to boiling. Reduce heat and simmer 5 minutes.

 Arrange spareribs on rack set over broiler pan. Combo cook at 75% microwave power and 300°F 25 minutes. Dip spareribs in sauce or brush sauce over spareribs; rotate. Combo cook at 75% microwave power and 300°F 10 minutes, brushing sauce over spareribs once.

 Arrange spareribs on rack set over broiler pan. Bake at 275°F 1 hour 15 minutes. Dip spareribs in sauce or brush sauce over spareribs and bake 30 minutes, brushing sauce over spareribs and rotating twice.

 Arrange spareribs on broiler pan. Combo cook at 75% microwave power and 350°F 25 minutes. Dip spareribs in sauce or brush sauce over spareribs and combo cook at 75% microwave power and 350°F 10 minutes, brushing sauce over spareribs once.

 Arrange spareribs on broiler pan. Bake at 325°F 1 hour 15 minutes. Dip spareribs in sauce or brush sauce over spareribs and bake 30 minutes, brushing sauce over spareribs once.

 Arrange spareribs on rack set over large microwave safe roasting pan. Cook at 75% microwave power 30 minutes. Dip spareribs in sauce or brush sauce over spareribs. Cook at 100% microwave power 10 minutes, brushing sauce over spareribs once.

Cranberry Pork Shoulder ____ 8 to 10 servings

5½- pound pork shoulder roast, bone-in
1 can (16 ounces) whole cranberry sauce
1 cup orange juice
1 teaspoon cinnamon
2 teaspoons salt
⅛ teaspoon ground cloves
½ teaspoon freshly ground pepper
Orange slices

Place roast in 4-quart casserole.* Combine cranberry sauce, orange juice, cinnamon, salt, cloves, and pepper; pour over roast. Cover casserole.

 Combo cook at 100% microwave power and 275°F 15 minutes. Reduce microwave power and combo cook at 50% microwave power and 275°F 1 hour 20 minutes, or until internal temperature reaches 170°F, turning roast over once. Slice roast and spoon cranberry sauce mixture over top. Garnish with orange slices.

 Bake at 275°F 3 hours, or until internal temperature reaches 170°F. Check occasionally and add a little more liquid, if needed. Slice roast and spoon cranberry sauce mixture over top. Garnish with orange slices.

 Combo cook at 100% microwave power and 325°F 15 minutes. Reduce microwave power and combo cook at 50% microwave power and 325°F 1 hour 20 minutes, or until internal temperature reaches 170°F, turning roast over once. Slice roast and spoon cranberry sauce mixture over top. Garnish with orange slices.

 Bake at 325°F 3 hours, or until internal temperature reaches 170°F. Check occasionally and add a little more liquid, if needed. Slice roast and spoon cranberry sauce mixture over top. Garnish with orange slices.

 Cook at 100% microwave power 20 minutes. Reduce power and cook at 50% microwave power 1 hour 30 minutes, or until internal temperature reaches 170°F, turning roast over once. Let stand, covered, 15 minutes before serving. Slice roast and spoon cranberry sauce mixture over top. Garnish with orange slices.

* In microwave method, be sure to use a microwave safe casserole.

Stuffed Pork Chops ——————— 6 servings

2 tablespoons vegetable oil
6 rib or loin chops,
    cut ¾-inch thick
    (about 2 pounds)
    Salt and freshly ground
    pepper
1 cup chopped fennel or
    celery
¼ cup chopped onion
2 cups fresh bread cubes
1 small apple, cored and
    chopped
⅓ cup chicken broth or dry
    white wine
½ teaspoon fennel seed,
    crushed

Heat oil in skillet. Brown chops lightly on both sides. Place in 9 × 13-inch baking dish.* Sprinkle with salt and pepper to taste. Add fennel and onion to skillet and sauté until onion is transparent. Remove from heat. Stir in bread cubes, apple, chicken broth, fennel seed, ½ teaspoon salt, and ¼ teaspoon pepper. Mix lightly until evenly moistened. Spoon onto chops in baking dish.

Preheat oven to 325°F. Total Cooking Time: 20 minutes. Combo cook at 75% microwave power and 325°F 10 minutes. Bake at 325°F 10 additional minutes, or until chops are tender and stuffing is lightly browned.

Bake at 300°F 45 minutes, or until chops are tender and stuffing is lightly browned, rotating once.

Preheat oven to 375°F. Total Cooking Time: 20 minutes. Combo cook at 70% microwave power and 375°F 10 minutes. Bake at 375°F 10 additional minutes, or until chops are tender and stuffing is lightly browned.

Bake at 350°F 45 minutes, or until chops are tender and stuffing is lightly browned.

Cook at 75% microwave power 14 minutes, or until chops are tender and stuffing is set.

* In microwave method, be sure to use a microwave safe baking dish.

Mustardy Pork Chops ———————— 6 servings

1 egg white
2 teaspoons prepared mustard
½ to ⅔ cup dry bread crumbs
½ teaspoon tarragon
½ teaspoon salt
6 shoulder pork chops (about
   2 pounds)
2 tablespoons vegetable oil
1 onion, sliced
1 cup dry white wine (¾ cup
   in microwave method)

Beat egg white, mustard, and 1 tablespoon water. Combine bread crumbs, tarragon, and salt. Dip chops in egg white mixture, then in bread crumb mixture, turning to coat both sides. Brown chops in hot oil in skillet. Place in shallow baking dish.* Sauté onion in drippings in skillet and spoon over chops. Pour wine around chops.

 Combo cook at 75% microwave power and 300°F 20 minutes, or until tender.

 Cover baking dish and bake at 275°F 1 hour, or until tender.

 Combo cook at 75% microwave power and 350°F 20 minutes, or until tender.

 Cover baking dish and bake at 325°F 1 hour, or until tender.

 Cover baking dish and cook at 75% microwave power 23 to 25 minutes until tender. Let stand 5 minutes before serving.

* In microwave method, be sure to use a microwave safe baking dish.

Fruit Curried Ham Steak ———— 6 servings

2 tablespoons butter or
    margarine, melted
2 tablespoons orange juice
1/4 cup firmly packed brown
    sugar
1 teaspoon curry powder
1/2 teaspoon salt
2 bananas
2 peaches
1 can (8 ounces) pineapple
    chunks, drained
2- pound smoked ham center
    slice, cut 1-inch thick
1/4 cup shredded coconut
    (optional)

Combine butter, orange juice, brown sugar, curry powder, and salt. Peel bananas and cut into 1-inch chunks. Peel and slice peaches. Add bananas, peaches, and pineapple to curry mixture. Stir to coat. Place ham in shallow baking dish.* Spoon fruit mixture over ham.

 Sprinkle coconut over fruit. Preheat oven to 325°F. Combo cook at 50% microwave power and 325°F 15 minutes, or until ham and fruit are hot and coconut is lightly browned.

 Sprinkle coconut over fruit. Bake at 300°F 35 minutes, or until ham and fruit are hot and coconut is lightly browned.

 Sprinkle coconut over fruit. Preheat oven to 375°F. Combo cook at 50% microwave power and 375°F 15 minutes, or until ham and fruit are hot and coconut is lightly browned.

 Sprinkle coconut over fruit. Bake at 350°F 35 minutes, or until ham and fruit are hot and coconut is lightly browned.

 Toast coconut and sprinkle over fruit. Cook at 75% microwave power 12 to 15 minutes until ham and fruit are hot. Let stand 3 minutes before serving.

* In microwave method, be sure to use a microwave safe baking dish.

Orange Spiced Ham _____ 12 to 16 servings

7- to 8-pound half ham shank
¾ cup orange marmalade
⅓ cup honey
½ teaspoon cinnamon
½ teaspoon ground cloves
2 tablespoons bourbon
2 oranges, thinly sliced
Whole cloves

Place ham on rack in large roasting pan.* Begin cooking as directed below. Remove ham from oven. Cut off skin and trim fat, leaving a thin layer. Combine marmalade, honey, cinnamon, and ground cloves. Cook over low heat until mixture melts and is smooth. Stir in bourbon. Brush some of the marmalade mixture generously over ham. Fasten orange slices to ham with whole cloves and wooden toothpicks, if needed. Brush slices generously with remaining marmalade mixture, and finish cooking as directed below.

 Combo cook at 75% microwave power and 300°F 50 minutes. Trim fat and cover with orange slices as directed above. Combo cook at 75% microwave power and 300°F 20 minutes, brushing with marmalade mixture twice.

 Bake at 300°F 1 hour 30 minutes. Trim fat and cover with orange slices as directed above. Bake at 300°F 30 minutes, brushing with marmalade mixture twice.

 Combo cook at 75% microwave power and 350°F 50 minutes. Trim fat and cover with orange slices as directed above. Combo cook at 75% microwave power and 350°F 20 minutes, brushing with marmalade mixture twice.

 Bake at 350°F 1 hour 30 minutes. Trim fat and cover with orange slices as directed above. Bake at 350°F 30 minutes, brushing with marmalade mixture twice.

 Cook at 75% microwave power 1 hour, rotating once. Trim fat and cover with orange slices as directed above. Cook at 75% microwave power 20 minutes, brushing with marmalade mixture twice.

* In microwave method, be sure to use a microwave safe roasting rack and pan.

Pork Chops and Spanish Rice — 4 servings

4 pork chops (about
   $1\frac{1}{2}$ pounds)
Salt and freshly ground
   pepper
1 large green pepper
1 cup long grain rice
1 onion, diced
1 can (8 ounces) tomato sauce

Place pork chops in shallow $2\frac{1}{2}$-quart casserole.* Sprinkle with salt and pepper to taste. Cut green pepper crosswise into four $\frac{1}{2}$-inch thick rings. Dice remaining green pepper. Place 1 green pepper ring on each pork chop. Sprinkle rice over chops. Combine diced green pepper, onion, tomato sauce, $1\frac{1}{2}$ cups water, and 1 teaspoon salt. Pour over chops and rice. Cover casserole.

 Combo cook at 100% microwave power and 325°F 10 minutes. Reduce microwave power and combo cook at 50% microwave power and 325°F 25 minutes, or until rice is tender.

 Bake at 300°F 1 hour 15 minutes, or until rice is tender.

 Combo cook at 100% microwave power and 375°F 10 minutes. Reduce microwave power and combo cook at 50% microwave power and 375°F 25 minutes, or until rice is tender.

 Bake at 350°F 1 hour 15 minutes, or until rice is tender.

 Cook at 100% microwave power 12 minutes. Reduce power and cook at 50% microwave power 30 minutes, or until rice is tender.

* In microwave method, be sure to use a microwave safe casserole.

Sausage Stuffed Pork Loin ____ 10 servings

4- pound boneless pork
   loin roast
½ pound bulk pork
   sausage
1 onion, minced
1 cup fresh bread crumbs
1 package (32 ounces)
   sauerkraut
1 cup dry white wine

Cut strings on pork roast and unroll. To increase surface of roast, slash "eye" of pork loin lengthwise and fold out flat. Brown sausage in skillet over moderate heat. Drain fat. Add onion and cook until tender. Remove from heat. Stir in bread crumbs. Spoon onto roast. Roll roast and retie with string. Rinse sauerkraut and place in large casserole.* Place roast over sauerkraut. Pour wine over roast. Cover casserole.

 Combo cook at 75% microwave power and 325°F 45 to 50 minutes until internal temperature reaches 170°F. Let stand 10 minutes before slicing. Slice and serve with sauerkraut.

 Bake at 300°F 2 to 2½ hours until internal temperature reaches 170°F, rotating once. Let stand 10 minutes before slicing. Slice and serve with sauerkraut.

 Combo cook at 75% microwave power and 375°F 45 to 50 minutes until internal temperature reaches 170°F. Let stand 10 minutes before slicing. Slice and serve with sauerkraut.

 Bake at 350°F 2 to 2½ hours until internal temperature reaches 170°F. Let stand 10 minutes before slicing. Slice and serve with sauerkraut.

 Cook at 75% microwave power 50 to 55 minutes until internal temperature reaches 170°F. Let stand 10 minutes before slicing. Slice and serve with sauerkraut.

* In microwave method, be sure to use a microwave safe casserole.

Butterflied Leg of Lamb ——— 10 to 12 servings

½ cup lemon juice
½ cup vegetable oil
¼ cup chopped fresh dill or
   2 tablespoons dried
   dillweed
1 large onion, minced
3 cloves garlic, minced
½ teaspoon freshly ground
   pepper
4½- pound boneless leg of lamb
   Cherry tomatoes, lemon
   wedges, and watercress

Combine lemon juice, oil, dill, onion, garlic, and pepper in large glass bowl. Add lamb and turn to coat. Cover and refrigerate at least several hours or overnight, turning lamb occasionally.

Place rack in 4th position from bottom. Preheat broiler 3 minutes. Place lamb on rack set over broiler pan. Total Cooking Time: 20 to 25 minutes. Combo cook at 50% microwave power and broil 10 minutes. Broil 10 to 15 additional minutes until lamb is desired doneness. Garnish with cherry tomatoes, lemon wedges, and watercress.

Place rack in 4th position from bottom. Preheat broiler 3 minutes. Place lamb on rack set over broiler pan. Broil 40 to 45 minutes, until lamb is desired doneness, rotating once. Garnish with cherry tomatoes, lemon wedges, and watercress.

Place rack in 4th position from bottom. Preheat broiler 3 minutes. Place lamb on broiler pan. Total Cooking Time: 18 to 20 minutes. Combo cook at 50% microwave power and broil 10 minutes. Broil 8 to 10 additional minutes until lamb is desired doneness. Garnish with cherry tomatoes, lemon wedges, and watercress.

Place rack in 3rd position from bottom. Preheat broiler 3 minutes. Place lamb on broiler pan and broil 20 minutes. Turn lamb and broil 20 to 25 minutes, until lamb is desired doneness. Garnish with cherry tomatoes, lemon wedges, and watercress.

Place lamb on rack over large microwave safe roasting pan. Cook at 75% microwave power 32 to 40 minutes until lamb is desired doneness. Garnish with cherry tomatoes, lemon wedges, and watercress.

Savory Lamb Casserole _____ 4 to 6 servings

1 large onion, sliced
1 pound lean ground lamb
  or beef
2/3 cup medium-size pre-cooked
  couscous, divided
1 can (10½ ounces)
  condensed chicken or
  beef broth, divided
1 teaspoon salt, divided
¼ teaspoon freshly ground
  pepper
3 tomatoes, diced
3 cups diced eggplant or
  zucchini
½ teaspoon coriander
1 small hot pepper, seeded
  and chopped
1 clove garlic, minced
1 small acorn squash,
  peeled, seeded, and
  cut into strips

Scatter onion in 3-quart casserole.* Combine lamb, 2 tablespoons couscous, ⅓ cup chicken broth, ½ teaspoon salt, and pepper. Shape into 1-inch balls. Place over onion. Add remaining couscous, tomatoes, and eggplant. Combine remaining broth, coriander, hot pepper, garlic, and remaining ½ teaspoon salt. Pour over ingredients in casserole. Top with squash and cover.

 Combo cook at 100% microwave power and 325°F 5 minutes. Reduce microwave power and combo cook at 50% microwave power and 325°F 15 minutes, or until vegetables are tender.

 Bake at 325°F 1 hour 30 minutes, or until vegetables are tender.

 Combo cook at 100% microwave power and 375°F 5 minutes. Reduce microwave power and combo cook at 50% microwave power and 375°F 15 minutes, or until vegetables are tender.

 Bake at 375°F 1 hour 30 minutes, or until vegetables are tender.

 Cook at 100% microwave power 8 minutes. Reduce power and cook at 75% microwave power 13 to 15 minutes until vegetables are tender.

* In microwave method, be sure to use a microwave safe casserole.

Lamb Kabobs ━━━━━━━━━━━━━ 6 servings

1½ pounds boneless lamb, cut
    into 1-inch cubes
½ cup dry red wine
¼ cup vegetable oil
1 teaspoon rosemary
1 teaspoon salt
2 cloves garlic, minced
6 small white onions
1 green pepper, seeded and
    cut into chunks
12 mushrooms
1 small zucchini, cut into
    6 pieces

Place lamb in large glass bowl. Combine wine, oil, rosemary, salt, and garlic. Pour over lamb. Cover and refrigerate at least 3 hours. Place onions in small microwave safe casserole with 2 tablespoons water. Cover and cook at 100% microwave power 2 to 3 minutes until slightly tender. Thread lamb and vegetables alternately on 12-inch skewers.* Place over 9×13-inch baking dish. Brush with some of the marinade.

MICROWAVE FIRST

Preheat oven to 400°F. Total Cooking Time: 10 to 11 minutes. Combo cook at 100% microwave power and 400°F 7 minutes. Brush with remaining marinade and bake at 400°F 3 to 4 additional minutes until lamb is lightly browned and desired doneness.

Preheat oven to 425°F. Bake 18 to 20 minutes until lamb is lightly browned and desired doneness, basting with remaining marinade twice.

MICROWAVE FIRST

Preheat oven to 450°F. Total Cooking Time: 12 to 13 minutes. Combo cook at 100% microwave power and 450°F 7 minutes. Turn and brush with remaining marinade and bake at 450°F 5 to 6 additional minutes until lamb is lightly browned and desired doneness.

Preheat broiler. Place skewers on broiler pan. Broil 10 minutes. Turn and brush with remaining marinade. Continue to broil 8 to 10 minutes until lamb is lightly browned and desired doneness.

Cook at 100% microwave power 10 to 12 minutes until lamb is desired doneness, brushing with remaining marinade twice.

*In microwave method, be sure to use wooden skewers and a microwave safe baking dish.

Lamb Curry _____ 6 servings

2 tablespoons vegetable oil
6 shoulder lamb chops (about 2¼ pounds)
1 large onion, sliced
1 green pepper, seeded and sliced
1 clove garlic, minced
1 can (16 ounces) tomatoes, cut up, liquid reserved
1 apple, cored and diced
½ cup raisins
4 to 5 teaspoons curry powder, or to taste
1 teaspoon salt
  Toasted sliced almonds

Heat oil in skillet. Brown chops lightly on both sides. Place in shallow casserole.* Sauté onion, green pepper, and garlic in drippings in skillet. Spoon over chops. Combine tomatoes with liquid, apple, raisins, curry powder, and salt. Spoon over chops and vegetables; cover.

 Combo cook at 50% microwave power and 300°F 30 minutes, or until chops are tender. Sprinkle with almonds and serve over hot rice, if desired.

 Bake at 275°F 2 hours, or until chops are tender. Check occasionally and add a little more liquid, if needed. Sprinkle with almonds and serve over hot rice, if desired.

 Combo cook at 50% microwave power and 350°F 30 minutes, or until chops are tender. Sprinkle with almonds and serve over hot rice, if desired.

 Bake at 325°F 2 hours, or until chops are tender. Check occasionally and add a little more liquid, if needed. Sprinkle with almonds and serve over hot rice, if desired.

 Cook at 50% microwave power 35 to 40 minutes until chops are tender. Sprinkle with almonds and serve over hot rice, if desired.

* In microwave method, be sure to use a microwave safe casserole.

Stuffed Breast of Veal ⎯⎯⎯⎯⎯⎯ 6 servings

1 breast of veal with pocket
   (2½ to 3 pounds)
4 tablespoons butter or
   margarine, divided
1 small onion, finely
   chopped
2 cups sliced mushrooms
1 clove garlic, minced
1½ cups cooked rice
½ teaspoon oregano
½ teaspoon salt
⅛ teaspoon freshly ground
   pepper
½ cup dry white wine
½ cup chicken broth

If necessary, cut pocket in veal. Loosen meat from rib bones along one side of veal with long sharp knife, leaving three sides uncut. Pull loosened edge up and continue cutting meat away from bones to within 1 inch of opposite side. Set aside. Heat 2 tablespoons butter in skillet. Sauté onion, mushrooms, and garlic until tender. Remove from heat. Stir in rice, oregano, salt, and pepper. Spoon into pocket of veal. Close opening with wooden toothpicks. Heat remaining 2 tablespoons butter in skillet. Brown veal lightly on both sides. Place in large casserole.* Add wine, broth, and 1 cup water (½ cup in microwave method). Cover casserole.

 Combo cook at 100% microwave power and 275°F 10 minutes. Reduce microwave power and combo cook at 50% microwave power and 275°F 1 hour, or until tender.

 Bake at 250°F 2½ to 3 hours, or until tender. Check halfway through cooking and add a little more chicken broth or water, if needed.

 Combo cook at 100% microwave power and 325°F 10 minutes. Reduce microwave power and combo cook at 50% microwave power and 325°F 1 hour, or until tender.

 Bake at 300°F 2½ to 3 hours, or until tender. Check halfway through cooking and add a little more chicken broth or water, if needed.

 Cook at 100% microwave power 13 minutes. Reduce power and cook at 75% microwave power 45 minutes, or until tender.

* In microwave method, be sure to use a microwave safe casserole.

Capered Veal Chops ──────── 4 servings

2 tablespoons butter or
  margarine
1½ pounds shoulder veal
  chops or steaks
¼ pound mushrooms, sliced
1 onion, sliced
1 cup chicken broth
2 tablespoons all-purpose
  flour
1 teaspoon salt
¼ teaspoon freshly ground
  pepper
1 bay leaf
½ cup dairy sour cream or
  heavy cream
2 tablespoons capers

Heat butter in skillet. Brown chops lightly on both sides. Arrange in shallow 2½-quart casserole.* Sauté mushrooms and onion in drippings in skillet until onion is transparent. Blend chicken broth, flour, salt, and pepper until smooth. Stir into mushroom mixture. Pour over chops. Add bay leaf and cover casserole.

 Combo cook at 75% microwave power and 300°F 20 minutes, or until tender. Remove chops to warm platter. Discard bay leaf and stir sour cream and capers into drippings in casserole. Spoon over chops and serve immediately.

 Bake at 275°F 1½ to 1¾ hours until tender. Check occasionally and add a little more liquid, if needed. Remove chops to warm platter. Discard bay leaf and stir sour cream and capers into drippings in casserole. Spoon over chops and serve immediately.

 Combo cook at 75% microwave power and 350°F 20 minutes, or until tender. Remove chops to warm platter. Discard bay leaf and stir sour cream and capers into drippings in casserole. Spoon over chops and serve immediately.

 Bake at 325°F 1½ to 1¾ hours until tender. Check occasionally and add a little more liquid, if needed. Remove chops to warm platter. Discard bay leaf and stir sour cream and capers into drippings in casserole. Spoon over chops and serve immediately.

 Cook at 75% microwave power 25 minutes, or until tender. Remove chops to warm platter. Discard bay leaf and stir sour cream and capers into drippings in casserole. Spoon over chops and serve immediately.

* In microwave method, be sure to use a microwave safe casserole.

Rosemary Veal Roast _____ 6 to 8 servings

2½- to 3-pound boneless veal
     shoulder roast
3 cloves garlic, slivered
1 tablespoon butter or
     margarine
1 tablespoon vegetable oil
1 onion, sliced
1 can (16 ounces) tomatoes,
     cut up
1 cup chicken broth (½ cup
     in microwave method)
2 teaspoons paprika
1½ teaspoons rosemary
1½ teaspoons salt
1 bay leaf

Cut slits in roast with sharp knife. Insert garlic slivers in slits. Heat butter and oil in skillet and brown roast on all sides. Place roast in 2½-quart casserole.* Sauté onion in drippings in skillet until transparent. Spoon over roast. Combine tomatoes, chicken broth, paprika, rosemary, and salt. Pour over roast. Add bay leaf. Cover casserole.

 Combo cook at 100% microwave power and 275°F 10 minutes. Reduce microwave power and combo cook at 50% microwave power and 275°F 35 to 40 minutes until internal temperature reaches 170°F and roast is tender. Let stand 5 minutes before carving. Discard bay leaf. Serve with tomato mixture spooned over roast.

 Bake at 250°F 1½ to 2 hours until internal temperature reaches 170°F and roast is tender. Let stand 5 minutes before carving. Discard bay leaf. Serve with tomato mixture spooned over roast.

 Combo cook at 100% microwave power and 350°F 10 minutes. Reduce microwave power and combo cook at 50% microwave power and 350°F 35 to 40 minutes until internal temperature reaches 170°F and roast is tender. Let stand 5 minutes before carving. Discard bay leaf. Serve with tomato mixture spooned over roast.

 Bake at 325°F 1½ to 2 hours until internal temperature reaches 170°F and roast is tender. Let stand 5 minutes before carving. Discard bay leaf. Serve with tomato mixture spooned over roast.

 Cook at 100% microwave power 10 minutes. Reduce power and cook at 50% microwave power 45 to 50 minutes until internal temperature reaches 170°F and roast is tender. Let stand 5 minutes before carving. Discard bay leaf. Serve with tomato mixture spooned over roast.

* In microwave method, be sure to use a microwave safe casserole.

Blanquette De Veau _____ 6 servings

6 tablespoons butter or margarine
6 tablespoons all-purpose flour
2½ pounds veal for stew, cut into 1-inch cubes
¾ pound small mushrooms
½ pound small white onions
¾ cup dry white wine
¾ cup chicken broth
1 carrot, cut in half
1 rib celery, cut in half
1 teaspoon thyme
1 teaspoon salt
1 bay leaf
1 egg yolk
½ cup heavy cream

Place butter in 2½- or 3-quart microwave safe casserole. Cook at 100% microwave power 1½ minutes, or until melted. Stir in flour until smooth. Add veal, mushrooms, onions, wine, chicken broth, carrot, celery, thyme, salt, and bay leaf. Cover casserole.

 Combo cook at 100% microwave power and 275°F 15 minutes. Reduce microwave power and combo cook at 50% microwave power and 275°F 45 minutes, or until veal is tender. Blend egg yolk and cream. Stir into stew. Bake at 275°F 5 minutes, or until sauce is thickened. Discard bay leaf. Stir and serve over hot noodles, if desired.

 Bake at 275°F 2 hours 30 minutes, or until veal is tender. Blend egg yolk and cream. Stir into stew. Bake at 275°F 5 minutes, or until sauce is thickened. Discard bay leaf. Stir and serve over hot noodles, if desired.

 Combo cook at 100% microwave power and 325°F 15 minutes. Reduce microwave power and combo cook at 50% microwave power and 325°F 45 minutes, or until veal is tender. Blend egg yolk and cream. Stir into stew. Bake at 325°F 5 minutes, or until sauce is thickened. Discard bay leaf. Stir and serve over hot noodles, if desired.

 Bake at 325°F 2 hours 30 minutes, or until veal is tender. Blend egg yolk and cream. Stir into stew. Bake at 325°F 5 minutes, or until sauce is thickened. Discard bay leaf. Stir and serve over hot noodles, if desired.

 Cook at 100% microwave power 15 minutes. Reduce power and cook at 75% microwave power 40 to 45 minutes until veal is tender. Blend egg yolk and cream. Stir into stew. Cook at 50% microwave power 2 to 3 minutes until sauce is thickened. Discard bay leaf. Stir and serve over hot noodles, if desired.

Oven-Fried Chicken _____ 6 servings

1/3 cup all-purpose flour
2 tablespoons grated
Parmesan cheese
1 1/2 teaspoons salt
1/4 teaspoon freshly ground
pepper
1 teaspoon oregano
1/2 teaspoon paprika
1/2 cup butter or margarine
6 chicken legs

Combine flour, cheese, salt, pepper, oregano, and paprika; set aside. Place butter in 2-cup glass measure and cook at 100% microwave power 1 to 1 1/2 minutes until melted. Pour into 10 × 15-inch jelly-roll pan.* Coat chicken lightly with melted butter, then with flour mixture. Arrange chicken in pan.

 Combo cook at 75% microwave power and 425°F 18 to 20 minutes until tender and browned, turning chicken once.

 Bake at 350°F 25 minutes. Turn chicken and bake 25 minutes, or until tender and browned.

 Combo cook at .75% microwave power and 450°F 18 to 20 minutes until tender and browned, turning chicken once. For additional crispness, bake at 450°F 5 minutes longer.

 Bake at 400°F 30 minutes. Turn chicken and bake 30 minutes, or until tender and browned. ·

 Cook at 75% microwave power 24 to 26 minutes, turning chicken after 12 minutes.

* In microwave method, use a 9 × 13-inch glass baking dish.

Coq au Vin _____ 4 servings

6 slices bacon, diced
¼ cup all-purpose flour
1 teaspoon salt
¼ teaspoon freshly ground
   pepper
3- pound broiler-fryer,
   quartered
½ pound small mushrooms
6 small white onions
1 cup dry red wine
1 clove garlic, minced

Fry bacon in skillet and drain on paper towels; set aside. Combine flour, salt, and pepper. Coat chicken with flour mixture. Brown lightly in drippings in skillet. Place chicken in 2½-quart casserole.* Top with mushrooms and onions. Add wine and garlic. Cover casserole.

 Combo cook at 75% microwave power and 325°F 20 minutes, or until chicken and onions are tender. Spoon into serving dish and sprinkle with crumbled bacon. Serve with hot rice or noodles, if desired.

 Bake at 300°F 50 to 60 minutes until chicken and onions are tender. Spoon into serving dish and sprinkle with crumbled bacon. Serve with hot rice or noodles, if desired.

 Combo cook at 75% microwave power and 375°F 20 minutes, or until chicken and onions are tender. Spoon into serving dish and sprinkle with crumbled bacon. Serve with hot rice or noodles, if desired.

 Bake at 350°F 50 to 60 minutes until chicken and onions are tender. Spoon into serving dish and sprinkle with crumbled bacon. Serve with hot rice or noodles, if desired.

 Cook at 100% microwave power 13 to 15 minutes until chicken and onions are tender. Spoon into serving dish and sprinkle with crumbled bacon. Serve with hot rice or noodles, if desired.

* In microwave method, be sure to use a microwave safe casserole.

Savory Chicken Stew —————— 6 servings

4½- to 5-pound roasting
chicken, cut up
½ pound carrots, cut into
chunks
½ pound small white onions
½ pound small mushrooms
1 cup chicken broth
½ cup heavy cream
⅓ cup all-purpose flour
2½ teaspoons salt
1½ teaspoons tarragon
Dumplings (page 142)
Chopped fresh parsley
(optional)

Place chicken in 4-quart casserole.* Add carrots, onions, and mushrooms, Blend chicken broth, cream, flour, salt, and tarragon. Pour over chicken. Cover casserole.

 Combo cook at 100% microwave power and 300°F 15 minutes. Reduce microwave power and combo cook at 40% microwave power and 300°F 25 to 30 minutes until tender. Prepare dumplings; drop on top of stew. Cook dumplings as directed on page 142. Sprinkle with parsley.

 Bake at 300°F 2½ to 3 hours, or until tender. Prepare dumplings; drop on top of stew. Cook dumplings as directed on page 142. Sprinkle with parsley.

 Combo cook at 100% microwave power and 350°F 15 minutes. Reduce microwave power and combo cook at 40% microwave power and 350°F 25 to 30 minutes until tender. Prepare dumplings; drop on top of stew. Cook dumplings as directed on page 142. Sprinkle with parsley.

 Bake at 350°F 2½ to 3 hours, or until tender. Prepare dumplings; drop on top of stew. Cook dumplings as directed on page 142. Sprinkle with parsley.

 Cook at 100% microwave power 18 minutes. Reduce power and cook at 75% microwave power 20 to 25 minutes until tender. Prepare dumplings; drop on top of stew. Cook dumplings as directed on page 142. Sprinkle with parsley.

* In microwave method, be sure to use a microwave safe casserole.

Chicken Kiev _____ 6 servings

½ cup butter, softened
2 tablespoons chopped fresh parsley
1 tablespoon chopped fresh dill
½ teaspoon tarragon
1 clove garlic, minced
3 boneless chicken breasts (about 1½ pounds), halved
2 tablespoons grated Romano cheese
2 tablespoons all-purpose flour
1 egg
1½ cups toasted fresh bread crumbs

Stir butter, parsley, dill, tarragon, and garlic until well mixed. Shape into a 2-inch square. Chill until firm. Place each chicken cutlet on waxed paper and pound to about ¼-inch thickness. Cut butter square into 6 pieces. Place one piece on each chicken cutlet. Fold long sides of chicken over butter, then roll, starting with pointed end and rolling toward wide end. Enclose butter completely. Combine cheese and flour. Beat egg and 1 teaspoon water. Coat chicken rolls with flour mixture, dip in egg, then in bread crumbs. Chill about 15 minutes to set coating. Place on greased baking sheet.*

MICROWAVE FIRST
Preheat oven to 425°F. Total Cooking Time: 8 minutes. Combo cook at 75% microwave power and 425°F 5 minutes. Bake at 425°F 3 additional minutes, or until browned and tender. Garnish with cherry tomatoes and watercress, if desired.

Preheat oven to 400°F. Bake 18 to 20 minutes until browned and tender, rotating once. Garnish with cherry tomatoes and watercress, if desired.

MICROWAVE FIRST
Preheat oven to 450°F. Total Cooking Time: 8 minutes. Combo cook at 75% microwave power and 450°F 5 minutes. Bake at 450°F 3 additional minutes, or until browned and tender. Garnish with cherry tomatoes and watercress, if desired.

Preheat oven to 425°F. Bake 18 to 20 minutes until browned and tender. Garnish with cherry tomatoes and watercress, if desired.

Cook at 100% microwave power 8 to 9 minutes until tender. Garnish with cherry tomatoes and watercress, if desired.

* In microwave method, be sure to use a microwave safe baking dish.

THE MAIN COURSE

Orange Glazed Cornish Hens — 6 servings

6 cornish hens (1 1/4 pounds each)
2 tablespoons butter or margarine
1 1/2 cups sliced mushrooms
2 1/2 cups cooked rice
1/2 cup sliced scallion
1/4 teaspoon grated orange zest
1 1/2 teaspoon salt, divided
1/4 teaspoon freshly ground pepper
  Paprika
2 tablespoons soy sauce
2 tablespoons sherry
2 tablespoons honey
1/4 cup thawed orange juice concentrate
1/2 teaspoon ground ginger

Rinse cornish hens. Pat dry and set aside. Heat butter in skillet. Sauté mushrooms until tender. Remove from heat and stir in rice, scallion, orange zest, 1 teaspoon salt, and pepper. Spoon mixture into hens. Tie legs with cotton string and sprinkle all over with salt and paprika, to taste. Place on rack in large roasting pan.* Combine soy sauce, sherry, honey, orange juice, ginger, and 1/2 teaspoon salt; set aside.

 Preheat oven to 375°F. Combo cook at 75% microwave power and 375°F 15 minutes. Brush with soy sauce mixture and combo cook at 75% microwave power and 375°F 10 minutes, or until glazed and tender, brushing with sauce twice.

 Preheat oven to 350°F. Bake 45 minutes, rotating once. Brush with soy sauce mixture and bake 15 minutes, or until glazed and tender, brushing with sauce twice.

 Preheat oven to 425°F. Combo cook at 75% microwave power and 425°F 15 minutes. Brush with soy sauce mixture and combo cook at 75% microwave power and 425°F 10 minutes, or until glazed and tender, brushing with sauce twice.

 Preheat oven to 400°F. Bake 45 minutes. Brush with soy sauce mixture and bake 15 minutes, or until glazed and tender, brushing with sauce twice.

 Cook at 100% microwave power 15 minutes. Brush with soy sauce mixture and cook at 100% microwave power 12 to 15 minutes until lightly browned and tender, brushing wtih sauce twice.

* In microwave method, be sure to use a microwave safe rack and roasting pan.

Gingered Duck _____ 4 servings

4- to 5-pound duckling
½ cup soy sauce
¼ cup firmly packed brown
   sugar
2 to 3 tablespoons grated
   fresh ginger or
   2 teaspoons ground
   ginger
1 tablespoon grated orange
   zest

Rinse duckling and drain well. Combine soy sauce, brown sugar, ginger, and orange zest in large glass bowl. Add duckling and marinate at least 3 hours or overnight. Remove duckling from marinade. Pierce skin several times with fork.

 Place duckling on rack in roasting pan. Preheat oven to 350°F. Combo cook at 75% microwave power and 350°F 28 to 45 minutes until internal temperature reaches 190°F, rotating and basting once or twice with marinade. Let stand 10 minutes before cutting into quarters.

 Place duckling on rack in roasting pan. Bake 2½ to 3 hours, or until internal temperature reaches 190°F, rotating and basting once or twice with marinade. Let stand 10 minutes before cutting into quarters.

 Place duckling on rack in roasting pan. Preheat oven to 400°F. Combo cook at 75% microwave power and 400°F 28 to 45 minutes until internal temperature reaches 190°F, basting once or twice with marinade. Let stand 10 minutes before cutting into quarters.

 Place duckling on rack in roasting pan. Bake 2½ to 3 hours, or until internal temperature reaches 190°F, basting once or twice with marinade. Let stand 10 minutes before cutting into quarters.

 Place duckling on microwave safe roasting rack in glass baking dish. Cook at 75% microwave power 40 to 60 minutes until internal temperature reaches 190°F, basting once or twice with marinade. Let stand 10 minutes before cutting into quarters.

Walnut-Stuffed Turkey ———————— 16 servings

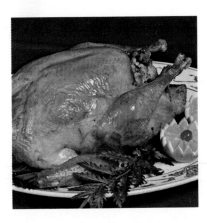

14- to 15-pound turkey
½ pound bulk pork sausage
2 onions, diced
4 cups fresh bread cubes
1 cup chopped walnuts
½ cup chopped fresh parsley
1½ teaspoons salt
½ teaspoon freshly ground
    pepper
2 eggs, beaten
½ cup butter or margarine,
    melted

Rinse turkey, drain, and set aside. Crumble sausage into large glass bowl. Cook at 100% microwave power 5 minutes, or until lightly browned. Drain fat. Stir in onions; cook at 100% microwave power 3 minutes. Stir in bread cubes, walnuts, parsley, salt, pepper, and eggs. Add 1 cup hot water and toss lightly to moisten. Spoon loosely into turkey cavity. Tie legs with string. Tuck neck skin under turkey and secure with wooden toothpick.

 Place turkey on rack in roasting pan. Brush with butter. Combo cook at 75% microwave power and 300°F 1 hour 30 minutes, or until internal temperature reaches 180°F to 185°F, rotating and basting with melted butter occasionally. Let stand 15 minutes before carving.

 Place turkey on rack in roasting pan. Brush with butter. Roast at 275°F 4½ to 5 hours, or until internal temperature reaches 180°F to 185°F, rotating and basting with melted butter occasionally. Let stand 15 minutes before carving.

 Place turkey on rack in roasting pan. Brush with butter. Combo cook at 75% microwave power and 350°F 1 hour 30 minutes, or until internal temperature reaches 180°F to 185°F, basting occasionally with melted butter. Let stand 15 minutes before carving.

 Place turkey on rack in roasting pan. Brush with butter. Roast at 325°F 4½ to 5 hours, or until internal temperature reaches 180°F to 185°F, basting occasionally with melted butter. Let stand 15 minutes before carving.

 Place turkey on microwave safe roasting rack in glass baking dish. Brush with butter. Cook at 75% microwave power 1 hour 45 minutes, or until internal temperature reaches 175°F, basting occasionally with melted butter. Let stand, covered, 20 minutes before carving

Chinese-Style Chicken _____ 6 servings

¼ cup butter or margarine
1 green pepper, seeded and
  cut into strips
¼ pound mushrooms, sliced
6 scallions
3 boneless chicken breasts
  (about 1½ pounds)
1 package (6 ounces) frozen
  pea pods, thawed
½ cup sliced water chestnuts
3 tablespoons dry sherry
3 tablespoons soy sauce
½ teaspoon ginger
½ teaspoon minced garlic
1 tablespoon cornstarch
  Hot cooked rice
1 can (3 ounces) chow mein
  noodles (optional)

Combine butter, green pepper, and mushrooms in 2-quart microwave safe casserole. Cut scallions lengthwise in half, then crosswise into 3-inch slices. Add to green pepper mixture. Cook at 100% microwave power 4 minutes, or until hot. Cut chicken into ¼-inch wide strips and add to green pepper mixture. Add pea pods and water chestnuts. Blend sherry, soy sauce, ginger, garlic, and cornstarch. Stir into chicken mixture. Cover casserole.

 Preheat oven to 375°F. Combo cook at 100% microwave power and 375°F 7 minutes, or until tender, stirring once. Stir, spoon over rice, and sprinkle with noodles.

 Preheat oven to 350°F. Bake 30 minutes, or until tender. Stir, spoon over rice, and sprinkle with noodles.

 Preheat oven to 425°F. Combo cook at 100% microwave power and 425°F 7 minutes, or until tender, stirring once. Stir, spoon over rice, and sprinkle with noodles.

 Preheat oven to 400°F. Bake 30 minutes, or until tender. Stir, spoon over rice, and sprinkle with noodles.

 Cook at 100% microwave power 8 to 9 minutes until tender, stirring once. Stir, spoon over rice, and sprinkle with noodles.

Shrimp Stuffed Fish ———————— 8 servings

5- to 6-pound whole salmon or
   red snapper, cleaned
   (cleaned weight about
   3½ to 4 pounds)
¼ cup olive oil
½ pound medium-size shrimp,
   shelled and deveined
1 onion, sliced
1 green pepper, seeded and
   sliced
2 cloves garlic, minced
1 tablespoon paprika
1 can (16 ounces) tomatoes,
   chopped
1 can (8 ounces) tomato sauce
½ cup dry white wine
½ teaspoon thyme
1 teaspoon salt
¼ teaspoon freshly ground
   pepper

Rinse fish and scrape skin to remove remaining scales. Rinse again and set aside. Heat oil in skillet. Sauté shrimp just until pink and curled. Remove shrimp from skillet with slotted spoon; set aside. Add onion, green pepper, garlic, and paprika to skillet; sauté until tender. Stir in remaining ingredients. Heat to simmering. Sprinkle fish cavity with salt and pepper and spoon some tomato mixture into fish. Place fish in large lightly greased roasting pan.* Spoon remaining tomato mixture over fish.

 Preheat oven to 350°F. Combo cook at 75% microwave power and 350°F 22 minutes, rotating and basting fish twice. Sprinkle shrimp over fish; stir. Combo cook at 100% microwave power and 350°F 4 minutes, or until fish flakes easily.

 Preheat oven to 325°F. Bake 50 minutes, rotating and basting fish 3 times. Sprinkle shrimp over fish; stir. Bake 10 to 15 minutes until fish flakes easily.

 Preheat oven to 400°F. Combo cook at 75% microwave power and 400°F 22 minutes, basting fish twice. Sprinkle shrimp over fish; stir. Combo cook at 100% microwave power and 400°F 4 minutes, or until fish flakes easily.

 Preheat oven to 375°F. Bake 50 minutes, basting fish 3 times. Sprinkle shrimp over fish; stir. Bake 10 to 15 minutes until fish flakes easily.

 Cook at 75% microwave power 24 minutes, basting fish twice. Sprinkle shrimp over fish; stir. Cook at 100% microwave power 5 to 6 minutes until fish flakes easily.

To serve, cut fish crosswise into 8 portions and top with tomato mixture. Garnish with lemon wedges, if desired.

* In microwave method, be sure to use a microwave safe roasting pan.

Shrimp Thermidor _____ 4 to 6 servings

1/4 cup butter or margarine
1 1/2 pounds large shrimp,
    shelled and deveined
1 onion, minced
1/4 cup all-purpose flour
1 3/4 cups half-and-half
1 tablespoon chopped fresh
    parsley
1/2 teaspoon tarragon
1/2 teaspoon paprika
1/2 cup dry white wine
2 egg yolks
1/2 teaspoon salt
1/4 teaspoon freshly ground
    pepper
2 tablespoons grated
    Parmesan cheese

Heat butter in skillet. Sauté shrimp just until pink and curled. Remove from skillet with slotted spoon. Add onion and sauté until transparent. Stir in flour until smooth. Blend in half-and-half, stirring rapidly to prevent lumping. Cook, stirring constantly, until thickened. Add parsley, tarragon, paprika, and wine; heat to simmering. Beat egg yolks lightly. Stir a little hot sauce into yolks, then rapidly stir yolk mixture back into sauce. Add salt and pepper. Stir in shrimp. Pour into 1 1/2-quart casserole.* Sprinkle with cheese.

 Preheat oven to 375°F. Combo cook at 50% microwave power and 375°F 8 minutes, or until lightly browned and bubbly. Serve over hot rice, if desired.

 Preheat oven to 350°F. Bake 15 to 20 minutes until lightly browned and bubbly. Serve over hot rice, if desired.

 Preheat oven to 425°F. Combo cook at 50% microwave power and 425°F 8 minutes, or until lightly browned and bubbly. Serve over hot rice, if desired.

 Preheat oven to 400°F. Bake 15 to 20 minutes until lightly browned and bubbly. Serve over hot rice, if desired.

 Cook at 75% microwave power 10 minutes, or until lightly browned and bubbly. Serve over hot rice, if desired.

* In microwave method, be sure to use a microwave safe casserole.

Flounder Turbans _____ 6 servings

6 fillets of sole or flounder
  (about 2 pounds)
½ cup sliced scallion
½ cup chopped fresh parsley
¾ cup fresh bread crumbs
1 teaspoon tarragon
1 teaspoon salt
½ teaspoon thyme
1 small clove garlic, minced
½ cup dry white wine, divided
¼ cup butter or margarine,
  melted, divided
Watercress
Lemon slices

Place fillets on flat surface. Combine scallion, parsley, bread crumbs, tarragon, salt, thyme, and garlic. Add 2 tablespoons wine and 1 tablespoon butter; toss to mix. Spoon a scant ¼ cup of mixture onto each fillet. Spread evenly over fillets. Starting with the tail end, roll up fillets and place each in a well greased 6-ounce custard cup. Pour 1 tablespoon wine into each cup. Brush each fillet generously with remaining butter. Place cups on small baking sheet for ease of handling.*

Preheat oven to 350°F. Total Cooking Time: 10 minutes. Combo cook at 100% microwave power and 350°F 5 minutes. Bake at 350°F 5 additional minutes, or until fish flakes easily. Let stand 3 to 4 minutes. Carefully lift fish from cups to warm serving platter. Garnish with watercress and lemon slices.

Preheat oven to 325°F. Bake 15 to 20 minutes until fish flakes easily. Let stand 3 to 4 minutes. Carefully lift fish from cups to warm serving platter. Garnish with watercress and lemon slices.

Preheat oven to 400°F. Total Cooking Time: 10 minutes. Combo cook at 100% microwave power and 400°F 5 minutes. Bake at 400°F 5 additional minutes, or until fish flakes easily. Let stand 3 to 4 minutes. Carefully lift fish from cups to warm serving platter. Garnish with watercress and lemon slices.

Preheat oven to 375°F. Bake 15 to 20 minutes until fish flakes easily. Let stand 3 to 4 minutes. Carefully lift fish from cups to warm serving platter. Garnish with watercress and lemon slices.

Cover cups with waxed paper. Cook at 100% microwave power 9 to 11 minutes until fish is opaque. Let stand 5 minutes. Carefully lift fish from cups to warm serving platter. Garnish with watercress and lemon slices.

* In microwave method, be sure to use a microwave safe baking dish.

Gingered Lime Fish Steaks —

½ cup sliced scallion
½ cup lime juice (about
   3 limes)
¼ cup vegetable oil
1½ teaspoons grated fresh
   ginger or 1 teaspoon
   ground ginger
1 teaspoon salt
2 pounds fish steaks, such
   as halibut, tile fish,
   or cod, cut about
   ¾-inch thick
Watercress
Lime wedges

Combine scallion, lime juice, oil, ginger, and salt in glass baking dish. Add fish and turn to coat. Cover and refrigerate at least several hours or overnight, turning fish occasionally. Drain fish.

MICROWAVE LAST

Place rack in 4th position from bottom. Preheat broiler 3 minutes. Arrange fish on rack set over broiler pan. Total Cooking Time: 8 minutes. Broil 4 minutes. Combo cook at 50% microwave power and broil 4 additional minutes, or until fish flakes easily, brushing with marinade once. Remove to warm serving platter and garnish with watercress and lime wedges.

Place rack in 4th position from bottom. Preheat broiler 3 minutes. Arrange fish on rack set over broiler pan. Broil 10 to 12 minutes until fish flakes easily, brushing with marinade once. Remove to warm serving platter and garnish with watercress and lime wedges.

MICROWAVE LAST

Place rack in 4th position from bottom. Preheat broiler 3 minutes. Arrange fish on broiler pan. Broil 4 minutes. Total Cooking Time: 8 minutes. Broil 4 minutes. Turn fish, brush with marinade, and combo cook at 50% microwave power and broil 4 additional minutes, or until fish flakes easily. Remove to warm serving platter and garnish with watercress and lime wedges.

Place rack in 4th position from bottom. Preheat broiler 3 minutes. Arrange fish on broiler pan. Broil 5 minutes. Turn fish, brush with marinade, and broil 5 to 6 minutes until fish flakes easily. Remove to warm serving platter and garnish with watercress and lime wedges.

Place fish in glass baking dish and cover with plastic wrap, leaving a vent in one corner. Cook at 100% microwave power 7 to 8 minutes until fish is opaque. Let stand, covered, 3 minutes. Remove to warm serving platter and garnish with watercress and lime wedges.

Light Delights

Turkey Tetrazzini _____ 6 servings

1 onion, sliced
½ pound mushrooms, sliced
⅓ cup butter or margarine
¼ cup all-purpose flour
1 cup half-and-half
1 can (10¾ ounces)
   condensed chicken broth
¼ cup dry sherry
   Salt and freshly ground
     pepper, to taste
½ pound spaghetti, cooked
3 cups diced cooked turkey
½ cup grated Parmesan cheese
   Red pepper, sliced
   (optional)

Place onion, mushrooms, and butter in 2½-quart glass bowl. Cook at 100% microwave power 6 minutes, stirring once. Stir in flour until smooth. Blend in half-and-half, chicken broth, sherry, salt, and pepper. Cook at 100% microwave power 9 minutes, or until thickened, stirring twice. Place spaghetti in greased 8×12-inch baking dish.* Scatter turkey over spaghetti, then top with sauce. Sprinkle with cheese and red pepper.

MICROWAVE
FIRST

Preheat oven to 325°F. Total Cooking Time: 18 to 20 minutes. Combo cook at 50% microwave power and 325°F 10 minutes. Bake at 325°F 8 to 10 additional minutes until lightly browned and bubbly.

Preheat oven to 300°F. Bake 35 minutes, or until browned and bubbly, rotating once.

MICROWAVE
FIRST

Preheat oven to 375°F. Total Cooking Time: 18 to 20 minutes. Combo cook at 50% microwave power and 375°F 10 minutes. Bake at 375°F 8 to 10 additional minutes until lightly browned and bubbly.

Preheat oven to 350°F. Bake 35 minutes, or until browned and bubbly.

Cook at 75% microwave power 11 to 12 minutes until bubbly.

* In microwave method, be sure to use a microwave safe baking dish.

LIGHT DELIGHTS

Chicken Pot Pie ─────────── 4 to 6 servings

1 can (10¾ ounces)
   condensed chicken broth
¼ pound mushrooms, sliced
1 cup diced carrots (about
   2 medium-size)
2 tablespoons cornstarch
½ teaspoon thyme
½ teaspoon oregano
1 package (10 ounces)
   frozen peas
2 cups diced cooked chicken
1½ cups biscuit mix
½ cup milk

Combine chicken broth, mushrooms, and carrots in 1½-quart microwave safe casserole. Cook at 100% microwave power 5 minutes, or until vegetables are tender. Blend cornstarch with 2 tablespoons water. Stir into hot vegetables. Add thyme and oregano. Stir in peas and chicken. Combine biscuit mix and milk; set aside.

Preheat oven to 350°F. Combo cook at 75% microwave power and 350°F 15 minutes. Spoon prepared biscuit topping over casserole. Bake at 350°F 10 minutes. Combo cook at 100% microwave power and 350°F 2 additional minutes, or until topping is done.

Cover casserole and bake at 325°F 40 minutes, or until simmering. Spoon prepared biscuit topping over casserole. Bake 20 minutes, or until topping is browned.

Preheat oven to 400°F. Combo cook at 75% microwave power and 400°F 15 minutes. Spoon prepared biscuit topping over casserole. Bake at 400°F 10 minutes. Combo cook at 100% microwave power and 400°F 2 additional minutes, or until topping is done.

Cover casserole and bake at 375°F 40 minutes, or until simmering. Spoon prepared biscuit topping over casserole. Bake 20 minutes, or until topping is browned.

Cook at 100% microwave power 13 minutes, stirring once. Spoon prepared biscuit topping over casserole and cook at 75% microwave power 6 minutes, or until topping is cooked and dry. Let stand 5 minutes before serving.

Monte Cristo Casserole _____ 6 servings

8 slices bread, buttered
   and cut into $\frac{1}{2}$-inch
   cubes
1 pound boiled ham, cubed
1$\frac{1}{2}$ cups shredded Swiss cheese
1 small onion, thinly sliced
1$\frac{1}{4}$ cups milk
3 eggs, beaten
1 tablespoon prepared
   mustard
   Salt and freshly ground
   pepper, to taste

Place bread in 2$\frac{1}{2}$-quart casserole* and combine with ham, cheese, and onion. Beat milk, eggs, and mustard until smooth. Stir into bread mixture. Sprinkle with salt and pepper.

 Preheat oven to 350°F. Combo cook at 75% microwave power and 350°F 15 minutes, or until casserole is set and top is lightly browned.

 Preheat oven to 300°F. Bake 45 to 50 minutes until casserole is set and top is lightly browned, rotating once.

 Preheat oven to 400°F. Combo cook at 75% microwave power and 400°F 15 minutes, or until casserole is set and top is lightly browned.

 Preheat oven to 350°F. Bake 45 to 50 minutes until casserole is set and top is lightly browned.

 Cook at 100% microwave power 14 to 15 minutes until center is almost set. Let stand directly on heat proof surface 5 minutes before serving.

* In microwave method, be sure to use a microwave safe casserole.

Mexicali Macaroni _____ 4 servings

½ pound bulk pork sausage
2 onions, diced
1 green pepper, seeded and
  diced
1 can (16 ounces) tomatoes,
  liquid reserved
1¼ teaspoons cumin or 2
  teaspoons chili powder
1 teaspoon oregano
1 teaspoon salt
1 cup uncooked elbow
  macaroni

Crumble sausage and place in 2-quart microwave safe casserole. Cook at 75% microwave power 8 to 10 minutes, stirring once. Drain excess fat. Add onions, green pepper, tomatoes with liquid, cumin, oregano, salt, macaroni, and 1 cup water (¾ cup in microwave method). Stir well. Cover casserole.

 Combo cook at 75% microwave power and 350°F 18 to 20 minutes until macaroni is tender. Top each serving with a dollop of sour cream, if desired.

 Bake at 325°F 1 hour 5 minutes to 1 hour 10 minutes until macaroni is tender. Top each serving with a dollop of sour cream, if desired.

 Combo cook at 75% microwave power and 400°F 18 to 20 minutes until macaroni is tender. Top each serving with a dollop of sour cream, if desired.

 Bake at 375°F 1 hour 5 minutes to 1 hour 10 minutes until macaroni is tender. Top each serving with a dollop of sour cream, if desired.

 Cook at 100% microwave power 5 minutes. Stir, cover, and cook at 50% microwave power 14 to 15 minutes until macaroni is tender. Top each serving with a dollop of sour cream, if desired.

Reuben Special ⸻ 4 servings

1 pound sauerkraut, drained
1 small apple, cored and
  chopped
1½ teaspoons caraway seed
¾ pound cooked corned beef
½ cup dry white wine
2 tablespoons brown sugar
1 tablespoon Dijon mustard
5 slices rye bread
  Butter or margarine
1 cup shredded Swiss cheese

Toss sauerkraut, apple, and caraway seed until mixed. Arrange in 8 × 12-inch baking dish.* Dice beef and spread over sauerkraut mixture. Combine wine, brown sugar, and mustard; pour over beef.

 Spread bread lightly with butter; dice and arrange over beef. Top with cheese. Preheat oven to 350°F. Combo cook at 75% microwave power and 350°F 15 minutes, or until bread is lightly browned.

 Spread bread lightly with butter; dice and arrange over beef. Top with cheese. Preheat oven to 325°F. Bake 25 minutes, or until bread is lightly browned, rotating once.

 Spread bread lightly with butter; dice and arrange over beef. Top with cheese. Preheat oven to 400°F. Combo cook at 75% microwave power and 400°F 15 minutes, or until bread is lightly browned.

 Spread bread lightly with butter; dice and arrange over beef. Top with cheese. Preheat oven to 375°F. Bake 25 minutes, or until bread is lightly browned.

 Toast bread and spread lightly with butter; dice and set aside. Cook casserole at 100% microwave power 1 minute. Let stand 2 to 3 minutes until cheese melts. Sprinkle with bread cubes.

* In microwave method, be sure to use a microwave safe baking dish.

Macaroni & Cheese _____ 6 servings

2 cups uncooked elbow macaroni
6 tablespoons butter or
   margarine, divided
1 cup half-and-half or
   light cream
1 teaspoon salt
¼ teaspoon freshly ground
   pepper
½ teaspoon dry mustard
1½ cups (6 ounces) shredded
   Cheddar cheese
½ cup fresh bread crumbs

Combine macaroni, 1¾ cups water, and 4 tablespoons butter in 2-quart microwave safe casserole. Cover and cook at 100% microwave power 9 minutes. Stir in half-and-half, salt, pepper, mustard, and cheese until smooth. Cover and cook at 50% microwave power 5 minutes; stir.

Sprinkle bread crumbs over casserole and dot with remaining 2 tablespoons butter. Preheat oven to 350°F. Total Cooking Time: 8 minutes. Combo cook at 50% microwave power and 350°F 5 minutes. Bake at 350°F 3 additional minutes, or until topping is lightly browned. Let stand 5 minutes before serving. Garnish with cherry tomatoes, if desired.

Sprinkle bread crumbs over casserole and dot with remaining 2 tablespoons butter. Preheat oven to 300°F. Bake 15 to 20 minutes until macaroni is tender and topping is lightly browned. Garnish with cherry tomatoes, if desired.

Sprinkle bread crumbs over casserole and dot with remaining 2 tablespoons butter. Preheat oven to 400°F. Total Cooking Time: 10 to 12 minutes. Combo cook at 50% microwave power and 400°F 5 minutes. Bake at 400°F 5 to 7 additional minutes until topping is lightly browned. Let stand 5 minutes before serving. Garnish with cherry tomatoes, if desired.

Sprinkle bread crumbs over casserole and dot with remaining 2 tablespoons butter. Preheat oven to 350°F. Bake 15 to 20 minutes until macaroni is tender and topping is lightly browned. Garnish with cherry tomatoes, if desired.

Toast bread crumbs in remaining 2 tablespoons butter in skillet over moderate heat. Sprinkle over casserole. Cook at 50% microwave power 8 to 9 minutes until macaroni is tender. Garnish with cherry tomatoes, if desired.

Texas Chili

1 package (16 ounces) pinto beans
2 pounds beef for stew, cut into ½-inch cubes
1 can (10½ ounces) condensed beef broth
1 large onion, chopped
3 tablespoons chili powder
3 tablespoons all-purpose flour
1½ teaspoons oregano
1½ teaspoons cumin
1 teaspoon salt
2 cloves garlic, minced
Red pepper strips

Rinse beans, pick over carefully, and rinse again. Cover with water and soak overnight. Drain well. Combine beans, beef, 2 cups water, and remaining ingredients in flameproof 4-quart casserole.*

 Cover casserole and combo cook at 100% microwave power and 275°F 20 minutes. Reduce microwave power and combo cook at 30% microwave power and 275°F 1 hour, or until beef and beans are tender. Garnish with red pepper strips.

 Heat on top of range until boiling. Cover casserole and bake at 275°F 2 to 2½ hours until beef and beans are tender. Garnish with red pepper strips.

 Cover casserole and combo cook at 100% microwave power and 325°F 20 minutes. Reduce microwave power and combo cook at 30% microwave power and 325°F 1 hour, or until beef and beans are tender. Garnish with red pepper strips.

 Heat on top of range until boiling. Cover casserole and bake at 325°F 2 to 2½ hours until beef and beans are tender. Garnish with red pepper strips.

 Cover casserole and cook at 100% microwave power 20 minutes. Reduce power and cook at 40% microwave power 1 hour to 1 hour 10 minutes until beef and beans are tender. Garnish with red pepper strips.

* In microwave method, be sure casserole is microwave safe as well as flameproof.

Chilies Rellenos Casserole _____ 6 servings

1 envelope (1¼ ounces)
   taco seasoning mix
1 pound lean ground beef
2 cans (4 ounces each) whole
   green chilies, drained,
   1 tablespoon liquid
   reserved
1 cup shredded Monterey
   Jack cheese
3 eggs, separated
3 tablespoons all-purpose
   flour
¼ teaspoon salt

Combine taco seasoning mix with beef as directed on package. Spoon into 2-quart casserole.* Split chilies, remove seeds, and cut into chunks. Arrange over beef mixture and top with cheese; set aside. Beat egg yolks, 1 tablespoon water, reserved chili liquid, flour, and salt until thickened. Beat egg whites until stiff peaks form; fold into egg yolk mixture. Spoon over cheese.

 Preheat oven to 375°F. Total Cooking Time: 8 minutes. Bake at 375°F 4 minutes. Combo cook at 50% microwave power and 375°F 4 additional minutes, or until topping is set and lightly browned.

 Preheat oven to 350°F. Bake 15 minutes, or until topping is set and lightly browned.

 Preheat oven to 425°F. Total Cooking Time: 8 minutes. Bake at 425°F 4 minutes. Combo cook at 50% microwave power and 425°F 4 additional minutes, or until topping is set and lightly browned.

 Preheat oven to 400°F. Bake 15 minutes, or until topping is set and lightly browned.

 Cook at 75% microwave power 8 minutes, or until topping is set. Let stand 5 minutes before serving.

*In microwave method, be sure to use a microwave safe casserole.

Pork and Leek Pie _____ 4 servings

4 leeks
1¼ pounds boneless pork cut
   into ½-inch cubes
1 apple, peeled, cored,
   and diced
1 teaspoon salt
½ teaspoon fennel seed
¼ teaspoon nutmeg
⅛ teaspoon freshly ground
   pepper
¾ cup chicken broth
1 tablespoon cornstarch
2 cups mashed potatoes

Cut tough green leaves off leeks. Split lengthwise and rinse well to remove sand. Slice ¼ inch thick. Place pork, leeks, apple, salt, fennel seed, nutmeg, and pepper in 2-quart casserole.* Combine chicken broth and cornstarch. Stir into pork mixture. Cover casserole.

MICROWAVE
FIRST

Preheat oven to 350°F. Total Cooking Time: 35 minutes. Combo cook at 50% microwave power and 350°F 25 minutes. Top with potatoes and bake, uncovered, at 350°F 10 additional minutes, or until potatoes are lightly browned.

Bake at 300°F 1 hour, or until tender. Top with potatoes and bake, uncovered, 10 minutes, or until potatoes are lightly browned.

MICROWAVE
FIRST

Preheat oven to 400°F. Total Cooking Time: 35 minutes. Combo cook at 50% microwave power and 400°F 25 minutes. Top with potatoes and bake, uncovered, at 400°F 10 additional minutes, or until potatoes are lightly browned.

Bake at 350°F 1 hour, or until tender. Top with potatoes and bake, uncovered, 10 minutes, or until potatoes are lightly browned.

Cook at 75% microwave power 15 to 17 minutes until tender. Top with potatoes and cook at 100% microwave power 4 to 5 minutes until hot.

* In microwave method, be sure to use a microwave safe casserole.

Stuffed Cabbage Leaves —————— 4 servings

8 large cabbage leaves
1 pound lean ground beef
1 can (15 ounces) tomato
  sauce, divided
1 onion, chopped
1/4 cup chopped green pepper
  (optional)
1/2 cup rolled oats
1 egg
1 1/2 teaspoons salt, divided
3/4 teaspoon oregano, divided
1/8 teaspoon freshly ground
  pepper

Place cabbage leaves in microwave safe casserole, add 1/4 cup water, cover, and cook at 100% microwave power 5 to 6 minutes until soft and pliable. Trim thick core end to make leaf thinner, if necessary. Combine beef, 1/4 cup water, 3/4 cup tomato sauce, onion, green pepper, oats, egg, 1 teaspoon salt, and 1/2 teaspoon oregano. Mix well. Divide mixture into 8 portions and place 1 portion on each cabbage leaf. Fold sides of leaf over beef mixture and, starting with core end of each leaf, roll up. Place, seam side down, in casserole. Combine remaining tomato sauce, 1/2 cup water, 1/2 teaspoon salt, 1/4 teaspoon oregano, and pepper. Pour over stuffed leaves; cover.

 Combo cook at 50% microwave power and 325°F 25 minutes, or until cabbage is tender and beef is cooked. Serve with sauce spooned over stuffed leaves.

 Bake at 300°F 1 hour 15 minutes, or until cabbage is tender and beef is cooked. Serve with sauce spooned over stuffed leaves.

 Combo cook at 50% microwave power and 375°F 25 minutes, or until cabbage is tender and beef is cooked. Serve with sauce spooned over stuffed leaves.

 Bake at 350°F 1 hour 15 minutes, or until cabbage is tender and beef is cooked. Serve with sauce spooned over stuffed leaves.

 Cook at 75% microwave power 25 to 30 minutes until cabbage is tender and beef is cooked. Serve with sauce spooned over stuffed leaves.

Sweet 'n Sour Stuffed Peppers — 6 servings

1 pound white fish fillets
Salt and freshly ground
  pepper
6 green peppers
1 onion, diced
3 tablespoons butter or
  margarine
1½ cups cooked rice
1 can (8 ounces) pineapple
  chunks, undrained
½ teaspoon ginger
1 tablespoon lemon juice

Place fillets in 6×10-inch glass baking dish; sprinkle with salt and pepper. Add ¼ cup water and cook at 100% microwave power 4 to 5 minutes until fish is opaque and flakes easily. Drain and flake fish; set aside. Slice tops off green peppers, remove seeds and membranes, and rinse. Place green peppers in glass baking dish, cover, and cook at 100% microwave power 4 minutes. Let stand, covered, 5 minutes. Dice green pepper tops and combine with onion and butter in microwave safe casserole. Cook at 100% microwave power 3 minutes, or just until tender. Stir in fish, rice, pineapple, ginger, lemon juice, and salt and pepper to taste. Spoon into green peppers and place in glass baking dish.

 Preheat oven to 325°F. Combo cook at 50% microwave power and 325°F 10 to 12 minutes until filling is hot.

 Preheat oven to 300°F. Add 1 cup water to baking dish. Bake 20 to 25 minutes until filling is hot.

 Preheat oven to 375°F. Combo cook at 50% microwave power and 375°F 10 to 12 minutes until filling is hot.

 Preheat oven to 350°F. Add 1 cup water to baking dish. Bake 20 to 25 minutes until filling is hot.

 Cook at 100% microwave power 8 to 10 minutes until filling is hot.

Pizza

½ pound sweet or hot
   Italian sausage links
1 pound frozen Italian
   bread dough, thawed
1¼ cups spaghetti sauce
1 large onion, sliced
1 large green pepper,
   seeded and sliced
2 to 3 cups sliced mushrooms
   (about ⅓ pound)
1 package (8 ounces)
   mozzarella cheese,
   shredded

Pierce sausage and place in small microwave safe casserole. Cover and cook at 100% microwave power 4 minutes. Let stand to cool. Cut into ¼-inch slices. Press dough into lightly greased 14-inch pizza pan or 10×15-inch jelly-roll pan. Let rise in warm place, free from draft, 10 minutes. Spread dough with spaghetti sauce; top with sausage, onion, green pepper, and mushrooms. Sprinkle with cheese.

Preheat oven to 375°F. Total Cooking Time: 14 to 16 minutes. Combo cook at 75% microwave power and 375°F 8 minutes. Bake at 375°F 6 to 8 additional minutes until lightly browned.

Preheat oven to 350°F. Bake 25 minutes, or until lightly browned and crisp, rotating once.

Preheat oven to 425°F. Total Cooking Time: 14 to 16 minutes. Combo cook at 75% microwave power and 375°F 8 minutes. Bake at 375°F 6 to 8 additional minutes until lightly browned.

Preheat oven to 400°F. Bake 25 minutes, or until lightly browned and crisp.

Not recommended.

Zucchini Moussaka ———————— 6 servings

1½ pounds zucchini
7 tablespoons butter or
   margarine, divided
1 pound lean ground beef
   or lamb
2 large onions, chopped
1 cup spaghetti sauce
½ cup dry red wine
   Salt and freshly ground
   pepper, to taste
3 tablespoons all-purpose
   flour
1½ cups half-and-half
½ cup grated Parmesan cheese

Cut zucchini lengthwise into ¼-inch slices. Heat 4 tablespoons butter in large skillet. Brown zucchini slices. Layer half the zucchini in 8- or 9-inch square baking dish.* Crumble beef into skillet. Add onions and sauté until beef is lightly browned. Drain fat. Stir in spaghetti sauce, wine, salt, and pepper. Simmer 10 minutes. Spoon over zucchini in baking dish. Top with remaining zucchini. Melt remaining 3 tablespoons butter in saucepan. Add flour and stir until smooth. Blend in half-and-half. Heat to boiling. Pour over ingredients in casserole. Sprinkle with cheese.

 Preheat oven to 325°F. Combo cook at 75% microwave power and 325°F 10 to 12 minutes until topping is set and lightly browned. Let stand 10 minutes before cutting.

 Preheat oven to 300°F. Bake 45 to 50 minutes until topping is set and lightly browned, rotating once. Let stand 10 minutes before cutting.

 Preheat oven to 375°F. Combo cook at 75% microwave power and 375°F 10 to 12 minutes until topping is set and lightly browned. Let stand 10 minutes before cutting.

 Preheat oven to 350°F. Bake 45 to 50 minutes until topping is set and lightly browned. Let stand 10 minutes before cutting.

 Cook at 75% microwave power 14 to 15 minutes until topping is set. Let stand 10 minutes before cutting.

* In microwave method, be sure to use a microwave safe baking dish.

Primavera Pie _____ 4 servings

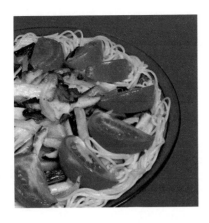

½ pound mushrooms, sliced
2 medium-size zucchini
   (about 1 pound), cut
   in julienne strips
1 large onion, sliced
3 tablespoons butter or
   margarine
1½ teaspoons oregano, divided
   Salt and freshly ground
   pepper, to taste
2 eggs, beaten
½ cup heavy cream
½ cup grated Parmesan cheese
½ pound spaghetti, cooked
   and drained
2 tomatoes, cut into wedges
1 cup shredded mozzarella
   cheese

Combine mushrooms, zucchini, onion, butter, and 1 teaspoon oregano in 2-quart microwave safe casserole. Cook at 100% microwave power 8 minutes, stirring once. Sprinkle with salt and pepper; set aside. Beat eggs, cream, Parmesan cheese, and remaining ½ teaspoon oregano. Stir in spaghetti; sprinkle with salt and pepper. Spoon spaghetti mixture evenly over bottom and sides of greased deep 10-inch pie plate.* Top with vegetable mixture and tomato wedges. Sprinkle with mozzarella cheese.

 Preheat oven to 325°F. Combo cook at 50% microwave power and 325°F 10 minutes, or until spaghetti mixture is set and cheese melts.

 Preheat oven to 300°F. Bake 25 minutes, or until spaghetti mixture is set and cheese melts.

 Preheat oven to 375°F. Combo cook at 50% microwave power and 375°F 10 minutes, or until spaghetti mixture is set and cheese melts.

 Preheat oven to 350°F. Bake 25 minutes, or until spaghetti mixture is set and cheese melts.

 Cook at 75% microwave power 10 minutes, or until spaghetti mixture is set and cheese melts. Let stand 5 minutes before serving.

* In microwave method, be sure to use a microwave safe pie plate.

Lasagna Bolognese ———————— 8 servings

1 pound lean ground beef
¼ pound mushrooms, sliced
1 onion, minced
¼ cup all-purpose flour
1 teaspoon basil
1 teaspoon oregano
1 teaspoon salt
1 can (13 ounces) evaporated
   milk, undiluted
1 can (8 ounces) tomato
   sauce
½ pound lasagna noodles,
   cooked
2 cups ricotta cheese
1 package (10 ounces) frozen
   chopped spinach, thawed
1 package (8 ounces)
   mozzarella cheese,
   shredded

Crumble beef into 1½-quart microwave safe casserole. Add mushrooms and onion. Cook at 100% microwave power 6 minutes, stirring twice. Drain fat. Stir in flour until smooth. Add basil, oregano, salt, milk, and tomato sauce; stir until smooth. Cook at 100% microwave power 7 minutes, or until thickened, stirring twice. Spoon 1 cup sauce into 9 × 13-inch baking dish.* Top with half the lasagna noodles. Spread ricotta cheese over noodles. Drain spinach well and spread over ricotta cheese. Top with half the mozzarella cheese and half the sauce. Complete layer with remaining noodles, sauce, and mozzarella cheese.

 Combo cook at 75% microwave power and 300°F 18 minutes, or until hot and bubbly.

 Bake at 300°F 40 to 45 minutes until hot and bubbly, rotating once.

 Combo cook at 75% microwave power and 350°F 18 minutes, or until hot and bubbly.

 Bake at 350°F 45 minutes, or until hot and bubbly.

 Cook at 75% microwave power 20 to 22 minutes until hot and bubbly. Let stand 10 minutes before serving.

* In microwave method, be sure to use a microwave safe baking dish.

Sausages and Peppers

2 pounds sweet Italian
   sausage links
3 green peppers, seeded and
   sliced
2 onions, sliced
1 can (15 ounces) tomato
   sauce
   Salt and freshly ground
   pepper, to taste
   Hot cooked spaghetti or
   split Italian rolls

Pierce sausages and place in 9×13-inch glass baking dish. Cook at 75% microwave power 10 minutes. Drain fat. To serve over spaghetti, cut sausages into 1-inch pieces. To serve in rolls, leave sausages whole. Add green peppers, onions, tomato sauce, salt, and pepper.

 Preheat oven to 325°F. Combo cook at 75% microwave power and 325°F 10 minutes, or until green peppers are tender. Stir well and serve as desired.

 Cover casserole and bake at 300°F 45 minutes, or until green peppers are tender. Stir well and serve as desired.

 Preheat oven to 375°F. Combo cook at 75% microwave power and 375°F 10 minutes, or until green peppers are tender. Stir well and serve as desired.

 Cover casserole and bake at 350°F 45 minutes, or until green peppers are tender. Stir well and serve as desired.

 Cook at 100% microwave power 8 minutes, or until green peppers and onions are tender. Stir well and serve as desired.

Puffy Oven Omelet _____ 2 servings

4 tablespoons butter or
    margarine, divided
1 small onion, sliced
½ small green pepper, sliced
½ small red pepper, sliced
½ teaspoon oregano
    Salt and freshly ground
    pepper, to taste
4 eggs, separated
½ cup shredded mozzarella or
    Monterey Jack cheese

Melt 2 tablespoons butter in small skillet. Add onion, green pepper, and red pepper; sauté about 5 minutes, or until tender. Add oregano, salt, and pepper. Stir; set aside. Place remaining 2 tablespoons butter in 9-inch microwave safe pie plate and cook at 75% microwave power about 1 minute; set aside. Beat egg yolks with salt and pepper until thick and lemon colored. Beat egg whites until stiff peaks form. Fold yolk mixture into whites with rubber spatula just until only a few white streaks show; do not overfold. Spoon into pie plate.

 Preheat oven to 375°F. Combo cook at 75% microwave power and 375°F 3 to 3½ minutes until tip of knife inserted in center comes out clean. Spoon filling onto half of omelet, sprinkle with cheese, fold over filling, and slide onto warm plate.

 Preheat oven to 325°F. Bake 8 to 10 minutes until tip of knife inserted in center comes out clean. Spoon filling onto half of omelet, sprinkle with cheese, fold over filling, and slide onto warm plate.

 Preheat oven to 400°F. Combo cook at 75% microwave power and 375°F 3 to 3½ minutes until tip of knife inserted in center comes out clean. Spoon filling onto half of omelet, sprinkle with cheese, fold over filling, and slide onto warm plate.

 Preheat oven to 350°F. Bake 10 minutes, or until tip of knife inserted in center comes out clean. Spoon filling onto half of omelet, sprinkle with cheese, fold over filling, and slide onto warm plate.

 Cook at 75% microwave power 3½ to 4½ minutes until tip of knife inserted in center comes out clean. Spoon filling onto half of omelet, sprinkle with cheese, fold over filling, and slide onto warm plate.

Cheese Soufflé _____ 6 servings

6 tablespoons butter or
   margarine
6 tablespoons all-purpose
   flour
¾ teaspoon fines herbes or
   thyme
¾ teaspoon salt
1 can (13 ounces) evaporated
   milk, undiluted
6 eggs, separated
1½ cups shredded Cheddar
   cheese

Melt butter in large saucepan. Stir in flour, fines herbes, and salt until smooth. Blend in milk. Cook, stirring constantly, until sauce is very thick and comes to a boil. Remove from heat. Stir in egg yolks, one at a time, beating quickly after each addition. Stir in cheese until melted and smooth. Beat egg whites until stiff peaks form. Stir a large spoonful of whites into cheese mixture. Gently fold remaining whites into cheese mixture; do not overfold. Pour into 2½-quart soufflé dish.

Preheat oven to 325°F. Total Cooking Time: 24 minutes. Combo cook at 75% microwave power and 325°F 4 minutes. Bake at 325°F 20 additional minutes, or until browned and well raised.

Preheat oven to 300°F. Bake 50 to 60 minutes until browned and well raised.

Preheat oven to 375°F. Total Cooking Time: 24 minutes. Combo cook at 75% microwave power and 375°F 4 minutes. Bake at 375°F 20 additional minutes, or until browned and well raised.

Preheat oven to 350°F. Bake 50 to 60 minutes until browned and well raised.

Not recommended.

Eggs in Avocados _____ 4 servings

2 large ripe avocados
2 tablespoons mild taco or
  chili sauce
4 eggs
  Salt and freshly ground
  pepper, to taste
1 large tomato, chopped
⅓ cup dairy sour cream or
  mayonnaise
1 tablespoon lemon juice
½ cup grated Cheddar cheese

Cut avocados in half, remove pits, enlarge hole slightly, and peel. Trim a thin slice from rounded side of avocado halves so they do not roll. Place, cut side up, in casserole.* Spoon ½ tablespoon taco sauce into each half. Break egg into each half and pierce yolks with toothpick. Sprinkle with salt and pepper.

 Preheat oven to 325°F. Combo cook at 50% microwave power and 325°F 12 to 15 minutes until eggs are desired doneness.

 Preheat oven to 325°F. Bake 25 to 30 minutes or until eggs are desired doneness.

 Preheat oven to 375°F. Combo cook at 50% microwave power and 375°F 12 to 15 minutes until eggs are desired doneness.

 Preheat oven to 375°F. Bake 25 to 30 minutes until eggs are desired doneness.

 Cook at 75% microwave power 12 to 14 minutes until eggs are desired doneness.

Spoon some of the tomato onto each avocado half. Combine sour cream and lemon juice; spoon over tomatoes. Sprinkle with cheese.

* In microwave method, be sure to use a microwave safe casserole.

Broccoli Quiche _____

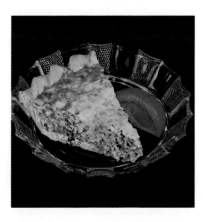

1 package (10 ounces) frozen
   chopped broccoli,
   thawed
1 9-inch unbaked pie shell
   (page 158)
1 cup shredded Swiss cheese
4 eggs
¾ teaspoon salt
¼ teaspoon freshly ground
   pepper
1½ cups half-and-half or
   heavy cream

Gently squeeze broccoli to extract excess liquid. Scatter broccoli in pie shell. (In microwave method, pre-cook pie shell as directed below.) Sprinkle with cheese. Beat eggs with salt and pepper.

 Beat half-and-half into eggs until well blended. Pour into pie shell. Preheat oven to 350°F. Combo cook at 75% microwave power and 350°F 13 to 15 minutes until tip of knife inserted in center comes out clean. Let stand 10 minutes before serving.

 Beat half-and-half into eggs until well blended. Pour into pie shell. Preheat oven to 400°F. Bake 10 minutes. Reduce temperature to 300°F and bake 25 minutes, or until tip of knife inserted in center comes out clean, rotating once. Let stand 10 minutes before serving.

 Beat half-and-half into eggs until well blended. Pour into pie shell. Preheat oven to 400°F. Combo cook at 75% microwave power and 400°F 13 to 15 minutes until tip of knife inserted in center comes out clean. Let stand 10 minutes before serving.

 Beat half-and-half into eggs until well blended. Pour into pie shell. Preheat oven to 425°F. Bake 15 minutes. Reduce temperature to 325°F and bake 35 minutes, or until tip of knife inserted in center comes out clean. Let stand 10 minutes before serving.

 Pre-bake crust conventionally in microwave safe pie plate or prick crust and cook at 100% microwave power 4½ to 5 minutes until crust is dry and opaque. Let stand to cool. Cook half-and-half in glass bowl at 100% microwave power 2½ to 3 minutes until steaming. Beat into eggs until well blended. Pour into pie shell. Cook at 75% microwave power 12 to 13 minutes until tip of knife inserted in center comes out clean. Let stand 10 minutes before serving.

Chili-Cheese Corn Bread _____ 6 servings

1 cup cornmeal
½ cup all-purpose flour
2 teaspoons baking powder
1 small onion, chopped
1 teaspoon salt
1 can (8 ounces) cream-style corn
1 can (4 ounces) chopped green chilies, undrained
⅓ cup milk
2 eggs, lightly beaten
3 tablespoons vegetable oil
6 fully cooked beef or pork sausage links, sliced
½ cup shredded Muenster cheese

Combine cornmeal, flour, baking powder, onion, and salt. Blend corn, chilies with liquid, milk, eggs, and oil. Stir into cornmeal mixture until combined. Add sausage and stir to mix. Pour into greased 9-inch square baking dish.* Sprinkle with cheese.

Preheat oven to 375°F. Total Cooking Time: 20 minutes. Combo cook at 50% microwave power and 375°F 16 minutes. Bake at 375°F 4 additional minutes, or until toothpick inserted in center comes out clean.

Preheat oven to 375°F. Bake 25 to 30 minutes until toothpick inserted in center comes out clean, rotating once.

Preheat oven to 425°F. Total Cooking Time: 21 minutes. Combo cook at 50% microwave power and 425°F 16 minutes. Bake at 425°F 5 additional minutes, or until toothpick inserted in center comes out clean.

Preheat oven to 425°F. Bake 25 to 30 minutes until toothpick inserted in center comes out clean.

Cook at 50% microwave power 18 to 19 minutes until center of top is dry to the touch. Let stand directly on heat proof surface 5 minutes before serving.

* In microwave method, be sure to use a microwave safe baking dish.

Sideliners

Orange-Carrots in Cream ———— 4 servings

1 pound carrots, peeled and
   shredded
2 tablespoons orange juice
2 tablespoons butter or
   margarine, melted
½ cup half-and-half
1 egg yolk
½ teaspoon salt
   Dash nutmeg
   Chopped fresh parsley

Combine carrots, orange juice, and butter in 3-cup microwave safe baking dish. Cover and cook at 100% microwave power 3 minutes. Blend half-and-half, egg yolk, salt, and nutmeg. Stir into carrot mixture.

 Combo cook at 30% microwave power and 275°F 7 to 8 minutes until set. Let stand 3 minutes. Garnish with parsley.

 Preheat oven to 300°F. Bake 15 minutes, or until set. Let stand 3 minutes. Garnish with parsley.

 Combo cook at 30% microwave power and 325°F 8 minutes, or until set. Let stand 3 minutes. Garnish with parsley.

 Preheat oven to 350°F. Bake 15 minutes, or until set. Let stand 3 minutes. Garnish with parsley.

 Cook at 50% microwave power 5 to 6 minutes until set. Let stand 3 minutes. Garnish with parsley.

Cream Cheese Spinach ———— 4 to 6 servings

2 packages (10 ounces each) frozen chopped spinach
4 ounces cream cheese (half of 8-ounce package)
3 eggs, beaten
1/3 cup half-and-half or milk
1 small onion, minced
1/2 teaspoon salt
1/4 teaspoon freshly ground pepper
1/8 teaspoon nutmeg
Sour cream (optional)

Place unopened packages of spinach on microwave safe plate and cook at 100% microwave power 5 minutes, or until thoroughly defrosted. Drain in colander, pressing out as much liquid as possible with back of spoon. Place half of each ingredient except sour cream in food processor bowl or blender container. Process until smooth. Repeat with remaining half of ingredients; combine both halves. Pour into greased 1½-quart casserole.*

 Preheat oven to 275°F. Combo cook at 75% microwave power and 275°F 15 to 18 minutes until knife inserted in center comes out clean. Garnish with sour cream.

 Preheat oven to 275°F. Place casserole in larger casserole. Add boiling water to come halfway up side of casserole. Bake 30 to 35 minutes until knife inserted in center comes out clean. Garnish with sour cream.

 Preheat oven to 325°F. Combo cook at 75% microwave power and 325°F 15 to 18 minutes until knife inserted in center comes out clean. Garnish with sour cream.

 Preheat oven to 325°F. Place casserole in larger casserole. Add boiling water to come halfway up side of casserole. Bake 30 to 35 minutes until knife inserted in center comes out clean. Garnish with sour cream.

 Cook at 50% microwave power 20 minutes, or until knife inserted in center comes out clean. Let stand 5 minutes before serving. Garnish with sour cream.

* In microwave method, be sure to use a microwave safe casserole.

Corn Pudding _____ 6 servings

2 cups milk or half-and-half
¼ cup butter or margarine
4 eggs
2 cups whole-kernel corn
6 slices bacon, cooked and
    crumbled, or ¼ cup
    minced ham
2 teaspoons sugar
½ teaspoon salt
⅛ teaspoon white pepper
2 tablespoons chopped fresh
    parsley

Combine milk and butter in 4-cup glass measure. Cook at 100% microwave power 2 to 3 minutes until steaming. Beat eggs lightly in bowl. Gradually beat in hot milk mixture. Stir in corn, bacon, sugar, salt, and pepper. Pour into greased 1½-quart casserole.*

 Combo cook at 50% microwave power and 275°F 16 to 17 minutes until knife inserted in center comes out clean. Let stand 10 minutes. Sprinkle with parsley.

 Place casserole in larger casserole. Add boiling water to come halfway up side of casserole. Bake at 275°F 1 hour, or until knife inserted in center comes out clean, rotating once. Let stand 10 minutes. Sprinkle with parsley.

 Combo cook at 50% microwave power and 325°F 16 to 17 minutes until knife inserted in center comes out clean. Let stand 10 minutes. Sprinkle with parsley.

 Place casserole in larger casserole. Add boiling water to come halfway up side of casserole. Bake at 325°F 1 hour, or until knife inserted in center comes out clean. Let stand 10 minutes. Sprinkle with parsley.

 Cook at 50% microwave power 18 to 19 minutes until knife inserted in center comes out clean. Let stand 10 minutes. Sprinkle with parsley.

* In microwave method, be sure to use a microwave safe casserole.

Corn and Tomato Scallop —— 6 to 8 servings

1 package (10 ounces) frozen whole-kernel corn
1 onion, thinly sliced
1 can (16 ounces) tomatoes, chopped, liquid reserved
1 teaspoon salt
¼ teaspoon freshly ground pepper
½ teaspoon oregano
1 cup fresh bread crumbs
½ cup shredded Cheddar cheese
2 tablespoons butter or margarine

Layer corn in greased 8×12-inch baking dish.* Top with onion, tomatoes, and reserved liquid. Combine salt, pepper, and oregano.

 Combine bread crumbs with seasoning mixture; sprinkle over ingredients in baking dish. Top with cheese and dot with butter. Preheat oven to 350°F. Combo cook at 100% microwave power and 350°F 10 minutes, or until onion is tender and topping is lightly browned.

 Combine bread crumbs with seasoning mixture; sprinkle over ingredients in baking dish. Top with cheese and dot with butter. Preheat oven to 325°F. Cover baking dish and bake 25 minutes. Remove cover and bake 10 to 15 minutes until onion is tender and topping is lightly browned.

 Combine bread crumbs with seasoning mixture; sprinkle over ingredients in baking dish. Top with cheese and dot with butter. Preheat oven to 400°F. Combo cook at 100% microwave power and 400°F 10 minutes, or until onion is tender and topping is lightly browned.

 Combine bread crumbs with seasoning mixture; sprinkle over ingredients in baking dish. Top with cheese and dot with butter. Preheat oven to 375°F. Cover baking dish and bake 25 minutes. Remove cover and bake 10 to 15 minutes until onion is tender and topping is lightly browned.

 Toast bread crumbs in butter in skillet over moderate heat; set aside. Sprinkle seasoning mixture over ingredients in baking dish. Cover cook at 100% microwave power 12 minutes. Sprinkle with bread crumbs and cheese. Let stand, uncovered, 5 minutes.

* In microwave method, be sure to use a microwave safe baking dish.

Baked Mushrooms _____ 4 to 6 servings

1 pound mushrooms, sliced
1 onion, minced
1 clove garlic, minced
¼ cup butter or margarine
1 tablespoon cornstarch
2 tablespoons dry sherry
1 teaspoon Dijon mustard
½ teaspoon Worcestershire
   sauce
½ teaspoon salt
1 cup fresh bread crumbs
   (toasted in microwave
   method)
1 tablespoon grated Parmesan
   cheese
Chopped fresh parsley

Combine mushrooms, onion, garlic, and butter in 1½-quart microwave safe casserole. Cover and cook at 100% microwave power 5 minutes. Combine cornstarch and sherry in small bowl; stir until smooth. Blend in mustard, Worcestershire, and salt. Add to mushroom mixture. Sprinkle with bread crumbs and cheese.

 Preheat oven to 350°F. Combo cook at 75% microwave power and 350°F 5 minutes, or until mushroom mixture is thickened and topping is lightly browned. Sprinkle with parsley.

 Preheat oven to 325°F. Bake 15 minutes, or until mushroom mixture is thickened and topping is lightly browned. Sprinkle with parsley.

 Preheat oven to 400°F. Combo cook at 75% microwave power and 400°F 5 minutes, or until mushroom mixture is thickened and topping is lightly browned. Sprinkle with parsley.

 Preheat oven to 375°F. Bake 15 minutes, or until mushroom mixture is thickened and topping is lightly browned. Sprinkle with parsley.

 Cook at 100% microwave power 4 minutes or until thickened. Sprinkle with parsley.

Barley-Mushroom Casserole _ 4 to 6 servings

¼ cup butter or margarine
1 onion, sliced
¼ pound mushrooms, sliced
1 cup medium-grain barley, rinsed
2 cups chicken or beef broth
1 bay leaf
¼ teaspoon rosemary
¾ teaspoon salt
¼ teaspoon freshly ground pepper
Chopped fresh parsley

Melt butter in medium-size skillet. Add onion and mushrooms; sauté 5 minutes, or until tender. Spoon into 2-quart casserole.* Add barley, chicken broth, bay leaf, rosemary, salt, and pepper; stir.

Total Cooking Time: 40 minutes. Combo cook at 100% microwave power and 300°F 10 minutes. Bake at 300°F 30 additional minutes, or until barley is tender. Remove bay leaf and sprinkle with parsley before serving.

Bake at 300°F 1 hour, or until barley is tender. Remove bay leaf and sprinkle with parsley before serving.

Total Cooking Time: 45 to 50 minutes. Combo cook at 100% microwave power and 350°F 10 minutes. Bake at 350°F 35 to 40 additional minutes until barley is tender. Remove bay leaf and sprinkle with parsley before serving.

Bake at 350°F 1 hour, or until barley is tender. Remove bay leaf and sprinkle with parsley before serving.

Cook at 100% microwave power 10 minutes. Stir, cover, and cook at 50% microwave power 25 minutes, or until barley is tender. Remove bay leaf and sprinkle with parsley before serving.

* In microwave method, be sure to use a microwave safe casserole.

Stuffed Onions ⸻⸻⸻ 6 servings

6 medium-size onions
1 cup fresh bread crumbs
½ cup chopped fresh parsley
1 tomato, peeled and chopped
2 tablespoons chopped pine nuts or almonds
1 clove garlic, minced
¼ teaspoon salt

Peel onions; cut off about ½ inch at stem end of each and trim root end close. Place in 8-inch round glass baking dish, add 2 tablespoons water, and cover. Cook at 100% microwave power 3 minutes, or until onions are somewhat tender. Let stand a few minutes to cool. Remove the center of each onion with a small spoon, leaving ¼-inch thick walls. (Reserve centers for use at another time.) Combine remaining ingredients. Spoon into onion shells. Place in baking dish; add 2 tablespoons water.

MICROWAVE FIRST

Preheat oven to 350°F. Total Cooking Time: 14 minutes. Combo cook at 75% microwave power and 350°F 4 minutes. Bake at 350°F 10 additional minutes, or until filling is slightly crusty and onions are tender.

Preheat oven to 325°F. Bake 20 minutes, or until filling is slightly crusty and onions are tender.

MICROWAVE FIRST

Preheat oven to 400°F. Total Cooking Time: 14 minutes. Combo cook at 75% microwave power and 400°F 4 minutes. Bake at 400°F 10 additional minutes, or until filling is slightly crusty and onions are tender.

Preheat oven to 375°F. Bake 20 minutes, or until filling is slightly crusty and onions are tender.

Cook at 75% microwave power 13 minutes, or until onions are tender.

Apple-Onion Bake ⸻ 4 to 6 servings

2 apples, peeled and sliced
2 onions, sliced
¼ cup firmly packed brown
    sugar
¼ cup raisins
½ teaspoon nutmeg
½ teaspoon salt
¼ cup apple juice
1 tablespoon butter or
    margarine

Layer half of the apples in 1-quart casserole.* Top with half of the onions. Combine brown sugar, raisins, nutmeg, and salt. Sprinkle half of the brown sugar mixture over onions. Repeat layers. Pour apple juice over ingredients in casserole and dot with butter.

 Preheat oven to 325°F. Combo cook at 100% microwave power and 325°F 5 to 6 minutes until apples and onions are tender.

 Cover casserole and bake at 300°F 40 to 45 minutes until apples and onions are tender.

 Preheat oven to 375°F. Combo cook at 100% microwave power 375°F 5 to 6 minutes until apples and onions are tender.

 Cover casserole and bake at 350°F 40 to 45 minutes until apples and onions are tender.

 Cover casserole and cook at 100% microwave power 7 minutes, or until apples and onions are tender. Let stand 5 minutes before serving.

*In microwave method, be sure to use a microwave safe casserole.

Parmesan Cauliflower _____ 6 servings

1 small head cauliflower
Salt, to taste
6 tablespoons grated Parmesan
    cheese
½ cup heavy cream
¾ cup fresh bread crumbs
2 tablespoons butter or
    margarine, melted
Toasted sliced almonds

Trim cauliflower and place in 1½-quart microwave safe casserole with 2 tablespoons water. Cover with plastic wrap, leaving vent in one corner, and cook at 100% microwave power 6 to 7 minutes until somewhat tender. Drain well. Break cauliflower into cauliflowerets and slice ½ inch thick. Layer ⅓ of the cauliflower in casserole. Sprinkle lightly with salt and 2 tablespoons cheese. Repeat layers twice. Pour cream over cauliflower.

 Top with bread crumbs and drizzle with butter. Preheat oven to 325°F. Combo cook at 100% microwave power and 325°F 6 to 7 minutes until cauliflower is tender and topping is lightly browned. Sprinkle with almonds before serving.

 Top with bread crumbs and drizzle with butter. Preheat oven to 300°F. Bake 20 to 25 minutes until cauliflower is tender and topping is lightly browned. Sprinkle with almonds before serving.

 Top with bread crumbs and drizzle with butter. Preheat oven to 375°F. Combo cook at 100% microwave power and 375°F 6 to 7 minutes until cauliflower is tender and topping is lightly browned. Sprinkle with almonds before serving.

 Top with bread crumbs and drizzle with butter. Preheat oven to 350°F. Bake 20 to 25 minutes until cauliflower is tender and topping is lightly browned. Sprinkle with almonds before serving.

 Toast bread crumbs in butter over moderate heat; set aside. Cover casserole and cook at 75% microwave power 8 minutes, or until tender. Sprinkle with almonds before serving.

Broccoli à la Swiss ——————— 6 to 8 servings

1 bunch broccoli (about
   1½ pounds)
1 cup half-and-half
3 eggs
½ teaspoon salt
¼ cup butter or margarine,
   melted
1 cup shredded Swiss cheese

Rinse broccoli and cut into spears. Arrange in 8 × 12-inch microwave safe baking dish. Add ¼ cup water and cover with plastic wrap, leaving vent in one corner. Cook at 100% microwave power 5 minutes, or until hot and almost tender. Drain water. Beat half-and-half, eggs, and salt in large bowl. Stir in butter and cheese; pour over broccoli.

 Preheat oven to 300°F. Combo cook at 50% microwave power and 300°F 6 to 7 minutes until cheese mixture is set and broccoli is tender.

 Preheat oven to 275°F. Bake 20 to 25 minutes until cheese mixture is set and broccoli is tender.

 Preheat oven to 350°F. Combo cook at 50% microwave power and 350°F 6 to 7 minutes until cheese mixture is set and broccoli is tender.

 Preheat oven to 325°F. Bake 20 to 25 minutes until cheese mixture is set and broccoli is tender.

 Cook at 50% microwave power 8 minutes, or until cheese mixture is set and broccoli is tender. Let stand 3 minutes before serving.

Creamed Cabbage ――――――――― 6 servings

6 cups coarsely diced cabbage
2 tablespoons butter or
   margarine
2 tablespoons all-purpose
   flour
1 teaspoon salt, or to taste
⅛ teaspoon freshly ground
   pepper
1 cup milk
3 to 4 tablespoons chopped
   fresh dill
1 cup fresh bread crumbs
⅓ cup shredded Swiss cheese

Place cabbage and 2 tablespoons water in 2-quart microwave safe casserole. Cook at 100% microwave power 7 minutes. Melt butter in saucepan. Stir in flour, salt, and pepper. Blend in milk. Cook, stirring, until thickened. Remove from heat and stir in dill. Pour over cabbage and stir to combine.

MICROWAVE FIRST Sprinkle with bread crumbs and cheese. Preheat oven to 350°F. Total Cooking Time: 12 minutes. Combo cook at 75% microwave power and 350°F 7 minutes. Bake at 350°F 5 additional minutes, or until topping is lightly browned.

Sprinkle with bread crumbs and cheese. Preheat oven to 325°F. Bake 20 minutes, or until topping is lightly browned.

MICROWAVE FIRST Sprinkle with bread crumbs and cheese. Preheat oven to 400°F. Total Cooking Time: 12 to 14 minutes. Combo cook at 75% microwave power and 400°F 7 minutes. Bake at 400°F 5 to 7 additional minutes, or until topping is lightly browned.

Sprinkle with bread crumbs and cheese. Preheat oven to 375°F. Bake 20 minutes, or until topping is lightly browned.

Toast bread crumbs in small skillet over moderate heat; set aside. Cook at 75% microwave power 9 minutes. Sprinkle with bread crumbs and cheese. Let stand 5 minutes, before serving.

Sauerkraut with Wine _____ 8 servings

6 slices bacon, sliced
2 onions, thinly sliced
1 clove garlic, minced
2 pounds sauerkraut, rinsed
   and drained
1 green pepper, seeded and
   sliced
1 cup dry white wine (¾ cup
   in microwave method)
1 bay leaf
½ teaspoon thyme
Salt and freshly ground
   pepper, to taste

Place bacon in shallow 2½-quart microwave safe casserole. Cook at 100% microwave power 7 minutes, stirring once. Remove bacon from casserole with slotted spoon. Add onion to casserole and cook at 100% microwave power 3 minutes. Stir in remaining ingredients until coated.

 Preheat oven to 350°F. Combo cook at 75% microwave power and 350°F 15 minutes, or until hot and bubbly. Remove bay leaf before serving.

 Cover casserole and bake at 300°F 1 hour, or until hot and bubbly. Remove cover and bake 10 minutes. Remove bay leaf before serving.

 Preheat oven to 400°F. Combo cook at 75% microwave power and 400°F 15 minutes, or until hot and bubbly. Remove bay leaf before serving.

 Cover casserole and bake at 350°F 1 hour, or until hot and bubbly. Remove cover and bake 10 minutes. Remove bay leaf before serving.

 Cook at 100% microwave power 5 minutes. Reduce power and cook at 50% microwave power 20 minutes, or until hot and bubbly. Remove bay leaf before serving.

Sesame Baked Eggplant  _____ 6 to 8 servings

1/4 cup sesame oil
1 onion, diced
2 tablespoons sesame seed
1 eggplant (1 pound), peeled and diced
1/4 pound mushrooms, sliced
1/3 cup soy sauce
1/2 teaspoon ginger
1 clove garlic, minced
1 1/2 teaspoons cornstarch (use in microwave method only)
Chopped fresh parsley

Combine oil, onion, and sesame seed in 2-quart microwave safe baking dish. Cook at 100% microwave power 5 minutes. Stir in eggplant and mushrooms until lightly coated with oil. Combine soy sauce, ginger, and garlic.

MICROWAVE FIRST

Pour soy sauce mixture over eggplant mixture; toss lightly. Total Cooking Time: 13 to 15 minutes. Combo cook at 100% microwave power and 350°F 5 minutes. Bake at 350°F 8 to 10 additional minutes until glazed and tender, stirring once. Sprinkle with parsley.

Pour soy sauce mixture over eggplant mixture; toss lightly. Bake at 350°F 35 to 40 minutes, stirring occasionally, until glazed and tender, stirring twice. Sprinkle with parsley.

MICROWAVE FIRST

Pour soy sauce mixture over eggplant mixture; toss lightly. Total Cooking Time: 15 to 17 minutes. Combo cook at 100% microwave power and 400°F 5 minutes. Bake at 400°F 10 to 12 additional minutes until eggplant is glazed and tender, stirring once. Sprinkle with parsley.

Pour soy sauce mixture over eggplant mixture; toss lightly. Bake at 400°F 35 to 40 minutes until glazed and tender, stirring twice. Sprinkle with parsley.

Stir cornstarch into soy sauce mixture. Pour over eggplant mixture; toss lightly. Cook at 100% microwave power 8 to 9 minutes until glazed and tender, stirring once. Sprinkle with parsley.

Scalloped Tomatoes _____ 4 to 6 servings

1 pound very ripe tomatoes,
   peeled and sliced
1 onion, thinly sliced
1 cup fresh bread crumbs
   (toasted in microwave
   method)
1/4 cup grated Parmesan cheese
1/2 teaspoon basil
1/2 teaspoon salt
1/8 teaspoon freshly ground
   pepper
2 tablespoons butter or
   margarine
Chopped scallions

Layer half of the tomatoes in lightly greased 1½-quart casserole,*. Top with half of the onions. Combine bread crumbs, Parmesan cheese, basil, salt, and pepper. Sprinkle half the crumb mixture over the onions. Repeat tomato and onion layers.

MICROWAVE FIRST

Sprinkle with remaining crumb mixture and dot with butter. Preheat oven to 350°F. Total Cooking Time: 15 minutes. Combo cook at 75% microwave power and 350°F 10 minutes. Bake at 350°F 5 additional minutes, or until topping is lightly browned. Sprinkle with scallions.

Sprinkle with remaining crumb mixture and dot with butter. Preheat oven to 350°F. Cover casserole and bake 40 minutes, or until hot and bubbly. Remove cover and bake 5 to 10 minutes until topping is lightly browned. Sprinkle with scallions.

MICROWAVE FIRST

Sprinkle with remaining crumb mixture and dot with butter. Preheat oven to 400°F. Total Cooking Time: 15 minutes. Combo cook at 75% microwave power and 400°F 10 minutes. Bake at 400°F 5 additional minutes, or until topping is lightly browned. Sprinkle with scallions.

Sprinkle with remaining crumb mixture and dot with butter. Preheat oven to 400°F. Cover casserole and bake 40 minutes, or until hot and bubbly. Remove cover and bake 5 to 10 minutes until topping is lightly browned. Sprinkle with scallions.

Dot with remaining 1 teaspoon butter. Cook at 100% microwave power 8 to 10 minutes until hot and bubbly. Let stand 5 minutes Sprinkle with remaining crumb mixture and scallions.

* In microwave method, be sure to use a microwave safe casserole.

Yellow Squash Bake ⸻ 6 servings

½ pound bulk pork sausage
¾ pound yellow squash,
    thinly sliced
  Salt and freshly ground
    pepper, to taste
1 onion, thinly sliced
1½ cups spaghetti sauce
1 cup cracker crumbs
2 tablespoons butter or
    margarine

Crumble sausage into 2-quart microwave safe casserole. Cook at 100% microwave power 4 minutes, stirring once. Remove sausage from casserole with slotted spoon; drain well. Layer half the squash in casserole. Sprinkle with salt and pepper. Top with half the onion and half the sausage. If spaghetti sauce is very thick add ¼ cup water and stir until combined. Spoon half the spaghetti sauce over onion. Top with half the cracker crumbs. Repeat layers. Dot with butter and cover casserole.

 Preheat oven to 350°F. Combo cook at 75% microwave power and 350°F 10 minutes. Remove cover and combo cook at 75% microwave power and 350°F 5 to 6 minutes until squash is tender and topping is lightly browned.

 Preheat oven to 325°F. Bake 45 minutes. Remove cover and bake 15 minutes, or until squash is tender and topping is lightly browned.

 Preheat oven to 400°F. Combo cook at 75% microwave power and 400°F 10 minutes. Remove cover and combo cook at 75% microwave power and 400°F 5 to 6 minutes until squash is tender and topping is lightly browned.

 Preheat oven to 375°F. Bake 45 minutes. Remove cover and bake 15 minutes, or until squash is tender and topping is lightly browned.

 Cook at 100% microwave power 11 to 12 minutes until squash is tender.

Ratatouille Casserole ———— 6 to 8 servings

2 tomatoes, chopped
2 cloves garlic, minced
⅓ cup chopped fresh parsley
1½ teaspoons salt
1 teaspoon basil
½ teaspoon thyme
¼ teaspoon freshly ground
   pepper
1 small eggplant (about
   ¾ pound), peeled and
   sliced
½ cup olive oil
2 small zucchini (about
   ¾ pound), sliced
2 small onions, sliced
1 small green pepper, seeded
   and sliced

Combine tomato, garlic, and parsley; set aside. Combine salt, basil, thyme, and pepper; set aside. Brown eggplant in hot oil in skillet. Remove eggplant from oil, reserving oil in skillet. Layer half the eggplant in 2-quart casserole.* Sprinkle with some of the seasoning mixture. Top with half the zucchini and sprinkle with some of the seasoning mixture. Sauté onions and green pepper in hot oil until tender. Spoon half of onion-green pepper mixture over zucchini. Sprinkle with some of the seasoning mixture and top with half of tomato mixture. Repeat layers with remaining ingredients.

 Combo cook at 50% microwave power and 350°F 23 to 25 minutes until vegetables are tender.

 Cover casserole and bake at 350°F 1 hour 15 minutes, or until vegetables are tender.

 Combo cook at 50% microwave power and 400°F 25 minutes, or until vegetables are tender.

 Cover casserole and bake at 400°F 1 hour 15 minutes, or until vegetables are tender.

 Cook at 75% microwave power 13 to 15 minutes until vegetables are tender.

* In microwave method, be sure to use a microwave safe casserole.

Zucchini-Mushroom Bake ___ 4 to 6 servings

3 slices bacon, diced
1 pound zucchini (2 medium-
    size), thinly sliced
¼ pound mushrooms, sliced
1 large tomato, diced
½ teaspoon salt, or to taste
¼ teaspoon freshly ground
    pepper
½ teaspoon oregano

Place bacon in 1½-quart glass casserole. Cook at 100% microwave power 3 minutes, stirring once. Remove bacon from casserole with slotted spoon; drain on paper towel. Stir zucchini, mushrooms, tomato, salt, pepper, and oregano into drippings in casserole. Cover casserole.

 Combo cook at 100% microwave power and 350°F 9 minutes, or until vegetables are tender. Stir and sprinkle with crumbled bacon before serving.

 Bake at 300°F 25 to 30 minutes until vegetables are tender. Stir and sprinkle with crumbled bacon before serving.

 Combo cook at 100% microwave power and 400°F 10 minutes, or until vegetables are tender. Stir and sprinkle with crumbled bacon before serving.

 Bake at 350°F 25 to 35 minutes until vegetables are tender. Stir and sprinkle with crumbled bacon before serving.

 Cook at 100% microwave power 10 minutes, or until vegetables are tender. Stir and sprinkle with crumbled bacon before serving.

Stuffed Zucchini Boats 6 servings

3 medium-size zucchini
   (about ½ pound each)
6 slices bacon, diced
1 onion, chopped
½ red pepper, diced
1 cup cooked rice
1 tablespoon vinegar
½ teaspoon basil
½ teaspoon salt
1 cup diced mozzarella or
   Monterey Jack cheese

Cut zucchini in half lengthwise. Scoop out centers with small spoon, leaving ¼-inch shells. Chop enough scooped out zucchini to make 1 cup. Place bacon in small microwave safe casserole. Cook at 100% microwave power 3 minutes. Add chopped zucchini, onion, and red pepper. Cook at 100% microwave power 3 to 4 minutes until onion is transparent. Stir in rice, vinegar, basil, salt, and cheese. Spoon into zucchini boats. Place in large shallow baking dish.*

 Preheat oven to 350°F. Combo cook at 75% microwave power and 350°F 8 to 10 minutes until zucchini is tender and filling is hot.

 Preheat oven to 350°F. Add 2 tablespoons hot water to baking dish. Cover with aluminum foil and bake 20 minutes. Uncover and bake 5 minutes, or until zucchini is tender and filling is hot.

 Preheat oven to 400°F. Combo cook at 75% microwave power and 400°F 9 to 10 minutes until zucchini is tender and filling is hot.

 Preheat oven to 400°F. Add 2 tablespoons hot water to baking dish. Cover with aluminum foil and bake 20 minutes. Uncover and bake 5 minutes, or until zucchini is tender and filling is hot.

 Cover with plastic wrap. Cook at 100% microwave power 8 to 10 minutes until zucchini is tender and filling is hot.

* In microwave method, be sure to use a microwave safe baking dish.

Sausage-Stuffed Squash _____ 4 servings

2 small acorn squash (about
   1 pound each)
¼ pound bulk pork sausage
   Salt and freshly ground
   pepper, to taste
2 scallions, sliced
½ cup heavy cream

Cut squash in half and scoop out seedy portion. Place cut-side down in large shallow microwave safe casserole. Add ¼ cup water and cook at 100% microwave power 10 minutes. Crumble sausage into small skillet; sauté until lightly browned; drain fat. Trim a thin slice from the bottom of each squash so halves will not roll. Return halves, cut-side up, to casserole. Sprinkle with salt and pepper. Spoon sausage into squash cavities and top with scallions. Fill cavities with cream.

 Combo cook at 75% microwave power and 350°F 8 to 10 minutes until tender.

 Bake at 300°F 35 to 40 minutes until tender.

 Combo cook at 75% microwave power and 400°F 8 to 10 minutes until tender.

 Bake at 350°F 40 to 45 minutes until tender.

 Cook at 50% microwave power 15 minutes, or until tender.

Sesame Soy Bok Choi _____ 6 servings

1 head bok choi or Chinese
   cabbage
5 scallions, halved
   lengthwise and cut
   into 1-inch pieces
¼ cup soy sauce
¼ cup dry white wine
2 tablespoons vegetable oil
2 teaspoons cornstarch
½ teaspoon ginger
½ teaspoon salt
1 clove garlic, minced
1 tablespoon sesame seed,
   toasted

Cut bok choi lengthwise into 4 pieces, then crosswise into 1½-inch pieces (about 8 cups). Place in 3- or 4-quart casserole.* Add scallions. Combine soy sauce, wine, oil, cornstarch, ginger, salt, and garlic in small bowl. Pour over bok choi and toss lightly to mix. Cover casserole.

 Preheat oven to 325°F. Combo cook at 100% microwave power and 325°F 7 to 8 minutes until crisp-tender. Toss lightly and sprinkle with sesame seed.

 Preheat oven to 300°F. Bake 25 to 30 minutes until crisp-tender. Toss lightly and sprinkle with sesame seed.

 Preheat oven to 375°F. Combo cook at 100% microwave power and 375°F 7 to 8 minutes until crisp-tender. Toss lightly and sprinkle with sesame seed.

 Preheat oven to 350°F. Bake 25 to 30 minutes until crisp-tender. Toss lightly and sprinkle with sesame seed.

 Cook at 100% microwave power 9 minutes, or until crisp-tender. Toss lightly and sprinkle with sesame seed.

*In microwave method, be sure to use a microwave safe casserole.

Brussels Sprouts and Grapes — 6 servings

1 pint Brussels sprouts
½ cup dry white wine
½ teaspoon salt
⅛ teaspoon freshly ground
    pepper
1½ cups seedless green grapes
2 egg yolks
1 tablespoon lemon juice

Clean Brussels sprouts. If necessary, cut very large sprouts in half to make all about the same size. Place in 1½-quart microwave safe casserole. Add wine, salt, and pepper. Cover and cook at 100% microwave power 5 to 6 minutes just until tender. Add grapes. Blend egg yolks and lemon juice. Stir into Brussels sprouts mixture.

 Preheat oven to 325°F. Combo cook at 50% microwave power and 325°F 3 to 4 minutes until sauce is thickened and grapes are hot. Stir before serving.

 Preheat oven to 300°F. Bake 10 minutes, or until sauce is thickened and grapes are hot. Stir before serving.

 Preheat oven to 375°F. Combo cook at 50% microwave power and 375°F 3 to 4 minutes until sauce is thickened and grapes are hot. Stir before serving.

 Preheat oven to 350°F. Bake 10 minutes, or until sauce is thickened and grapes are hot. Stir before serving.

 Cook at 50% microwave power 5 minutes, or until sauce is thickened and grapes are hot. Stir before serving.

Swiss Braised Endive _____ 6 servings

3 large Belgian endive
¼ cup sliced scallion
¼ cup chicken broth
¼ cup heavy cream or
   half-and-half
2 teaspoons all-purpose
   flour
¼ teaspoon salt
   Dash nutmeg
¾ cup fresh bread crumbs
½ cup shredded Swiss cheese
   Chopped fresh parsley

Trim endive. Cut lengthwise in half and place in 8 × 12-inch microwave safe baking dish. Sprinkle with scallion. Add chicken broth. Cover with plastic wrap, leaving vent in one corner, and cook at 100% microwave power 4 to 5 minutes until almost tender. Blend cream, flour, salt, and nutmeg until smooth. Pour over endive.

Sprinkle with bread crumbs and cheese. Preheat oven to 350°F. Total Cooking Time: 10 minutes. Combo cook at 50% microwave power and 350°F 3 minutes. Bake at 350°F 7 additional minutes, or until topping is lightly browned and sauce is hot. Garnish with parsley.

Sprinkle with bread crumbs and cheese. Preheat oven to 350°F. Bake 15 to 20 minutes until topping is lightly browned and sauce is hot. Garnish with parsley.

Sprinkle with bread crumbs and cheese. Preheat oven to 400°F. Total Cooking Time: 10 minutes. Combo cook at 50% microwave power and 400°F 3 minutes. Bake at 400°F 7 additional minutes, or until topping is lightly browned and sauce is hot. Garnish with parsley.

Sprinkle with bread crumbs and cheese. Preheat oven to 400°F. Bake 15 to 20 minutes until topping is lightly browned and sauce is hot. Garnish with parsley.

Toast bread crumbs in small skillet over moderate heat; set aside. Cover baking dish with plastic wrap, leaving vent in one corner. Cook at 50% microwave power 7 to 8 minutes until sauce is hot. Uncover and sprinkle with bread crumbs and cheese. Cook at 100% microwave power 1 minute to melt cheese. Garnish with parsley.

Deviled Leeks _____ 4 to 6 servings

6 large leeks
¼ cup butter or margarine,
   melted, divided
⅓ cup chicken broth or water
¼ cup dry white wine
1 teaspoon salt
⅛ teaspoon freshly ground
   pepper
2 teaspoons Dijon mustard
½ teaspoon thyme
1 cup fresh bread crumbs

Clean leeks; cut lengthwise into 4 pieces, then crosswise into 1-inch strips. Place in 1½-quart casserole.* Combine 2 tablespoons butter, chicken broth, wine, salt, and pepper. Pour over leeks; set aside. Combine remaining butter, mustard, and thyme.

MICROWAVE FIRST

Add bread crumbs to butter mixture and toss lightly to mix. Sprinkle crumb mixture over leeks. Preheat oven to 350°F. Total Cooking Time: 11 minutes. Combo cook at 100% microwave power and 350°F 6 minutes. Bake at 350°F 5 additional minutes, or until topping is lightly browned and leeks are tender.

Add bread crumbs to butter mixture and toss lightly to mix. Sprinkle crumb mixture over leeks. Preheat oven to 300°F. Cover casserole and bake 20 minutes. Remove cover and bake 5 to 6 minutes until topping is lightly browned and leeks are tender.

MICROWAVE FIRST

Add bread crumbs to butter mixture and toss lightly to mix. Sprinkle crumb mixture over leeks. Preheat oven to 400°F. Total Cooking Time: 11 minutes. Combo cook at 100% microwave power and 400°F 6 minutes. Bake at 400°F 5 additional minutes, or until topping is lightly browned and leeks are tender.

Add bread crumbs to butter mixture and toss lightly to mix. Sprinkle crumb mixture over leeks. Preheat oven to 350°F. Cover casserole and bake 20 minutes. Remove cover and bake 5 to 6 minutes until topping is lightly browned and leeks are tender.

Cover casserole and cook at 100% microwave power 8 to 9 minutes until leeks are tender. Let stand 5 minutes. Brown bread crumbs in 2 tablespoons butter in small skillet over moderate heat. Add mustard and thyme and toss lightly to mix. Sprinkle crumb mixture over leeks.

* In microwave method, be sure to use a microwave safe casserole.

Rosemary Turnip Puff _____ 4 to 6 servings

1 pound turnips, peeled and
    cut into chunks
1/4 cup butter or margarine,
    divided
1/4 cup heavy cream or
    half-and-half
1 egg, lightly beaten
1/2 teaspoon rosemary
1/4 teaspoon salt
3/4 cup fresh bread crumbs

Place turnips in 1-quart microwave safe casserole. Cover and cook at
100% microwave power 5 minutes. Let stand 5 minutes; drain. Process
in food processor or mash with potato masher. Return to casserole. Stir
in 2 tablespoons butter until melted. Add cream, egg, rosemary, and salt;
stir until mixed.

MICROWAVE
FIRST

Place remaining 2 tablespoons butter in small glass bowl; cook
at 100% microwave power 1 minute, or until melted. Stir in
bread crumbs and sprinkle over turnip mixture. Preheat oven to
350°F. Total Cooking Time: 13 minutes. Combo cook at 50%
microwave power and 350°F 8 minutes. Bake at 350°F 5
additional miinutes, or until topping is lightly browned.

Place remaining 2 tablespoons butter in small glass bowl; cook
at 100% microwave power 1 minute, or until melted. Stir in
bread crumbs and sprinkle over turnip mixture. Preheat oven to
275°F. Bake 30 to 35 minutes until turnip mixture is set and
topping is lightly browned.

MICROWAVE
FIRST

Place remaining 2 tablespoons butter in small glass bowl; cook
at 100% microwave power 1 minute, or until melted. Stir in
bread crumbs and sprinkle over turnip mixture. Preheat oven to
400°F. Total Cooking Time: 13 minutes. Combo cook at 50%
microwave power and 400°F 8 minutes. Bake at 400°F 5
additional minutes, or until topping is lightly browned.

Place remaining 2 tablespoons butter in small glass bowl; cook
at 100% microwave power 1 minute, or until melted. Stir in
bread crumbs and sprinkle over turnip mixture. Preheat oven to
325°F. Bake 30 to 35 minutes until turnip mixture is set and
topping is lightly browned.

Toast bread crumbs in remaining 2 tablespoons butter in skillet
over moderate heat; set aside. Cook at 75% microwave power
casserole 8 to 9 minutes until turnip mixture is set. Sprinkle with
crumb mixture.

Baked Beans _____ 8 servings

1 pound navy pea beans
2 onions, chopped
½ cup firmly packed brown
   sugar
½ cup molasses
1½ teaspoons salt
¾ teaspoon dry mustard
6 slices bacon, diced

Rinse beans well. Pick over and rinse again. Place in 3- or 4-quart casserole.* Add 4½ cups water (4 cups in microwave method). Cover and let stand at least several hours or overnight. Do not drain. Cover casserole.

 Combo cook at 100% microwave power and 275°F 12 minutes. Reduce microwave power and combo cook at 30% microwave power and 275°F 25 minutes. Stir in remaining ingredients, cover, and combo cook at 30% microwave power and 275°F 50 minutes, or until beans are tender and glazed, stirring once.

 Bake at 300°F 1 hour. Stir in remaining ingredients, cover, and bake 1 hour 30 minutes. Stir and bake, uncovered, 1 hour, or until beans are tender and glazed.

 Combo cook at 100% microwave power and 325°F 12 minutes. Reduce microwave power and combo cook at 30% microwave power and 325°F 25 minutes. Stir in remaining ingredients, cover, and combo cook at 30% microwave power and 325°F 50 minutes, or until beans are tender and glazed, stirring once.

 Bake at 350°F 1 hour. Stir in remaining ingredients, cover, and bake 1 hour 30 minutes. Stir and bake, uncovered, 1 hour, or until beans are tender and glazed.

 Cook at 100% microwave power 14 minutes. Reduce power and cook at 30% microwave power 30 minutes. Stir in remaining ingredients, cover, and cook at 100% microwave power 5 minutes, then cook at 40% microwave power 45 minutes, or until beans are tender.

* In microwave method, be sure to use a microwave safe casserole.

Red Cabbage and Beets _____ 6 servings

3 medium-size beets
4 cups red cabbage,
   shredded
1 small onion, sliced
¼ cup vinegar
1 tablespoon cornstarch
1 teaspoon salt
¼ teaspoon cinnamon
⅛ teaspoon ground cloves
½ cup dairy sour cream
   (optional)

Scrub beets and place in microwave safe casserole with ¼ cup water. Cover and cook at 100% microwave power 5 minutes. Let stand 5 minutes. Drain beets; peel and cut into julienne strips. Combine beets, cabbage, and onion in 4-quart casserole.* Blend ⅓ cup water, vinegar, cornstarch, salt, cinnamon, and cloves until smooth. Pour over beet mixture and stir to mix. Cover.

 Combo cook at 75% microwave power and 300°F 13 minutes, or until cabbage is tender, stirring once. Fold sour cream into cooked vegetables or pass at table.

 Bake at 300°F 50 minutes, or until cabbage is tender, stirring once. Fold sour cream into cooked vegetables or pass at table.

 Combo cook at 75% microwave power and 350°F 13 minutes, or until cabbage is tender, stirring once. Fold sour cream into cooked vegetables or pass at table.

 Bake at 350°F 50 minutes, or until cabbage is tender, stirring once. Fold sour cream into cooked vegetables or pass at table.

 Cook at 100% microwave power 10 minutes, or until cabbage is tender, stirring once. Fold sour cream into cooked vegetables or pass at table.

* In microwave method, be sure to use a microwave safe casserole.

Cheese-Potato Bake _____ 6 servings

1½ pounds baking potatoes (about 3)
½ cup heavy cream or half-and-half
½ cup dairy sour cream
2 eggs, beaten
½ teaspoon salt
¼ teaspoon freshly ground pepper
¼ cup sliced scallion, divided
¾ cup shredded Swiss cheese, divided

Pierce potatoes with fork. Cook at 100% microwave power 10 to 12 minutes until tender. Let stand 5 minutes. Peel and cut into ¼-inch thick slices. Combine heavy cream, sour cream, eggs, salt, and pepper. Layer ⅓ of the potatoes in greased 1½ -quart casserole.* Sprinkle with 2 tablespoons each scallion and cheese. Spoon a little sour cream mixture over top. Top with remaining potatoes. Pour remaining sour cream mixture over ingredients in casserole and sprinkle with remaining scallion and cheese.

Preheat oven to 300°F. Total Cooking Time: 15 to 17 minutes. Combo cook at 50% microwave power and 300°F 5 minutes. Bake at 300°F 10 to 12 additional minutes until hot and center is almost set.

Preheat oven to 300°F. Bake 25 to 30 minutes until hot and center is almost set.

Preheat oven to 350°F. Total Cooking Time: 15 to 17 minutes. Combo cook at 50% microwave power and 350°F 5 minutes. Bake at 350°F 10 to 12 additional minutes until hot and center is almost set.

Preheat oven to 350°F. Bake 25 to 30 minutes until hot and center is almost set.

Cook at 50% microwave power 12 to 14 minutes until hot and center is almost set.

* In microwave method, be sure to use a microwave safe casserole.

Stuffed Potatoes ———————————— 6 servings

6 medium-size potatoes
 (about 2 pounds)
3 tablespoons butter or
 margarine
⅓ to ½ cup milk
¼ cup grated Parmesan cheese
2 tablespoons sliced scallion
1 egg
1 teaspoon salt
⅛ teaspoon freshly ground
 pepper

Scrub potatoes, pierce with fork, and cook as directed below. Cut a slit in each potato and carefully scoop out pulp into mixer bowl. Cut off a small amount of potato skin around slit to make boat shape; reserve shells. Add butter and milk to mixer bowl; beat until fluffy. Add cheese, scallion, egg, salt, and pepper; beat until well combined. Spoon mixture into shells.

Combo cook potatoes at 100% microwave power and 375°F 13 minutes, or until tender. Assemble as directed above. Total Cooking Time: 11 minutes. Combo cook at 100% microwave power and 375°F 3 minutes. Bake at 375°F 8 additional minutes, or until lightly browned.

Bake potatoes at 400°F 40 minutes, or until fork tender. Assemble as directed above. Bake filled potatoes at 350°F 15 minutes, or until lightly browned.

Combo cook potatoes at 100% microwave power and 425°F 13 minutes, or until tender. Assemble as directed above. Total Cooking Time: 11 minutes. Combo cook at 100% microwave power and 425°F 3 minutes. Bake at 425°F 8 additional minutes, or until lightly browned.

Bake potatoes at 450°F 40 minutes, or until tender. Assemble as directed above. Bake filled potatoes at 400°F 15 minutes, or until lightly browned.

Cook potatoes at 100% microwave power 14 to 15 minutes until tender. Assemble as directed above. Cook filled potatoes at 100% microwave power 5 to 6 minutes until hot.

Dilled Potato Puff _____ 4 to 6 servings

4 medium-size potatoes
   (about 1¼ pounds)
½ cup half-and-half
2 tablespoons butter or
   margarine
½ cup shredded Swiss cheese
3 eggs, separated
1 tablespoon chopped fresh
   dill or ¾ teaspoon
   dried dill
½ teaspoon salt, or to taste

Peel potatoes and dice. Place in 2-quart microwave safe casserole. Add ½ cup water; cover and cook at 100% microwave power 10 to 12 minutes until very tender; drain well. Force through a ricer or mash until very smooth. Beat in half-and-half, butter, cheese, egg yolks, dill, and salt. Beat egg whites until stiff peaks form. Fold into potato mixture. Pour into greased 1½-quart casserole or soufflé dish.

 Preheat oven to 375°F. Total Cooking Time: 15 minutes. Combo cook at 75% microwave power and 375°F 5 minutes. Bake at 375°F 10 additional minutes, or until puffed and set.

 Preheat oven to 350°F. Bake 20 to 25 minutes until puffed and set.

 Preheat oven to 425°F. Total Cooking Time: 15 minutes. Combo cook at 75% microwave power and 425°F 5 minutes. Bake at 425°F 10 additional minutes, or until puffed and set.

 Preheat oven to 400°F. Bake 20 to 25 minutes until puffed and set.

 Not recommended.

Hashed Brown Potatoes

1 pound potatoes, peeled and
    shredded (about 2 cups)
1 small onion, grated
4 tablespoons butter or
    margarine, melted,
    divided
½ teaspoon salt
¼ teaspoon freshly ground
    pepper

Rinse shredded potatoes, squeeze out as much liquid as possible, then pat dry with paper towels. Combine potatoes, onion, 2 tablespoons butter, salt, and pepper. Pour remaining 2 tablespoons butter into 9-inch pie plate or quiche dish; tilt to spread evenly. Spoon potato mixture evenly on pie plate.

Preheat oven to 400°F. Total Cooking Time: 15 to 20 minutes. Combo cook at 75% microwave power and 400°F 10 minutes. Bake at 400°F 5 to 10 additional minutes until crisp and lightly browned.

Preheat oven to 375°F. Bake 35 to 40 minutes until crisp and lightly browned, rotating once.

Preheat oven to 450°F. Total Cooking Time: 15 to 20 minutes. Combo cook at 75% microwave power and 450°F 10 minutes. Bake at 375°F 5 to 10 additional minutes until crisp and lightly browned.

Preheat oven to 425°F. Bake 35 to 40 minutes until crisp and lightly browned.

Not recommended.

Hot German Potato Salad —— 6 to 8 servings

6 slices bacon, diced
2 pounds potatoes, peeled
   and sliced
1 large onion, sliced
½ cup beef broth
1¼ teaspoons salt
½ teaspoon freshly ground
   pepper
1 teaspoon dry mustard
⅓ cup cider vinegar
¼ cup chopped dill pickle
1 tablespoon brown sugar
Chopped fresh parsley
Sliced radishes

Place bacon in shallow 2-quart microwave safe casserole. Cook at 100% microwave power 3 to 5 minutes until browned. Remove bacon from casserole with slotted spoon; drain and set aside. Add potatoes and onion to drippings in casserole and toss lightly to coat. Combine beef broth, salt, pepper, and mustard; pour over potato mixture. Combine vinegar, pickle, and brown sugar; set aside.

 Preheat oven to 350°F. Combo cook at 75% microwave power and 350°F 10 to 11 minutes until potatoes are tender but firm. Pour pickle mixture over potato mixture; stir gently to combine. Let stand at least 20 minutes. Sprinkle with reserved bacon, parsley, and radishes before serving. Serve warm or at room temperature.

 Cover casserole with aluminum foil and bake at 375°F 40 to 45 minutes until potatoes are tender but firm. Pour pickle mixture over potato mixture; stir gently to combine. Let stand at least 20 minutes. Sprinkle with reserved bacon, parsley, and radishes before serving. Serve warm or at room temperature.

 Preheat oven to 375°F. Combo cook at 75% microwave power and 375°F 10 to 12 minutes until potatoes are tender but firm. Pour pickle mixture over potato mixture; stir gently to combine. Let stand at least 20 minutes. Sprinkle with reserved bacon, parsley, and radishes before serving. Serve warm or at room temperature.

 Cover casserole with aluminum foil and bake at 400°F 40 to 45 minutes until potatoes are tender but firm. Pour pickle mixture over potato mixture; stir gently to combine. Let stand at least 20 minutes. Sprinkle with reserved bacon, parsley, and radishes before serving. Serve warm or at room temperature.

 Cook at 100% microwave power 12 minutes, or until potatoes are tender but firm. Pour pickle mixture over potato mixture; stir gently to combine. Let stand at least 20 minutes. Sprinkle with reserved bacon, parsley, and radishes before serving. Serve warm or at room temperature.

Maple-Sweet Potato Puff _____ 6 servings

1½ pounds sweet potatoes
4 eggs, separated
½ cup maple syrup
2 tablespoons butter or
    margarine
¾ teaspoon salt
¼ teaspoon nutmeg
¼ cup chopped salted
    peanuts or pecans

Pierce potatoes with fork and cook at 100% microwave power 7 to 8 minutes until tender. Let stand 5 minutes. Peel potatoes and mash until smooth. Beat in egg yolks, maple syrup, butter, salt, and nutmeg. Beat egg whites until stiff peaks form. Fold into sweet potato mixture. Spoon into greased 2-quart soufflé dish or casserole.* Sprinkle peanuts around edge.

 Combo cook at 50% microwave power and 275°F 10 minutes, or until knife inserted in center comes out clean.

 Bake at 300°F 45 to 50 minutes until knife inserted in center comes out clean, rotating once.

 Combo cook at 50% microwave power and 325°F 10 minutes, or until knife inserted in center comes out clean.

 Bake at 350°F 45 to 50 minutes until knife inserted in center comes out clean.

 Cook at 50% microwave power 12 minutes, or until knife inserted near center comes out clean. Let stand 5 minutes before serving.

* In microwave method, be sure to use a microwave safe soufflé dish or casserole.

Spiced Brown Rice _____ 6 servings

¼ pound mushrooms, sliced
1 onion, chopped
1 small green pepper, seeded and chopped
1 clove garlic, minced
¼ cup butter or margarine
2 cups chicken broth
1 cup brown rice
1 teaspoon salt
½ teaspoon thyme
½ teaspoon freshly ground pepper

Combine mushrooms, onion, green pepper, garlic, and butter in microwave safe casserole. Cover and cook at 100% microwave power 7 minutes, or until vegetables are tender, stirring once. Stir in remaining ingredients and cover casserole.

 Combo cook at 100% microwave power and 300°F 5 minutes. Reduce microwave power and combo cook at 40% microwave power and 300°F 25 minutes, or until rice is tender.

 Bake at 300°F 1 hour 15 minutes, or until rice is tender.

 Combo cook at 100% microwave power and 350°F 5 minutes. Reduce microwave power and combo cook at 40% microwave power and 350°F 25 to 30 minutes until rice is tender.

 Bake at 350°F 1 hour and 15 minutes, or until rice is tender.

 Cook at 50% microwave power 35 to 40 minutes until rice is tender, stirring once.

Baked Rice _____ 6 servings

¼ cup butter or margarine
¼ cup minced onion
1 clove garlic, minced
1½ cups long grain rice
2½ cups chicken broth
1 bay leaf
¾ teaspoon salt
⅛ teaspoon freshly ground
  pepper
⅓ cup grated Parmesan
  cheese (optional)
Cherry tomatoes and fresh
  parsley

Combine butter, onion, and garlic in 2-quart microwave safe casserole. Cook at 100% microwave power 2 minutes. Stir in rice. Cook at 100% microwave power 3 minutes. Stir in chicken broth, bay leaf, salt, and pepper. Cover casserole.

 Combo cook at 100% microwave power and 325°F 5 minutes. Reduce microwave power and combo cook at 50% microwave power and 325°F 8 to 10 minutes until liquid is absorbed. Remove bay leaf. Sprinkle with cheese and garnish with cherry tomatoes and parsley.

 Preheat oven to 350°F. Bake 20 to 22 minutes until liquid is absorbed. Remove bay leaf. Sprinkle with cheese and garnish with cherry tomatoes and parsley.

 Combo cook at 100% microwave power and 375°F 5 minutes. Reduce microwave power and combo cook at 50% microwave power and 375°F 8 to 10 minutes until liquid is absorbed. Remove bay leaf. Sprinkle with cheese and garnish with cherry tomatoes and parsley.

 Preheat oven to 400°F. Bake 20 to 22 minutes until liquid is absorbed. Remove bay leaf. Sprinkle with cheese and garnish with cherry tomatoes and parsley.

 Cook at 100% microwave power 5 minutes. Reduce power and cook at 50% microwave power 10 to 12 minutes until liquid is absorbed. Remove bay leaf. Sprinkle with cheese and garnish with cherry tomatoes and parsley.

Onion-Noodle Kugel _____ 8 servings

2 medium-size onions, sliced
¼ cup butter or margarine
2 cups dairy sour cream
3 eggs, slightly beaten
¼ cup grated Parmesan cheese
1½ teaspoons salt
¼ teaspoon freshly ground
    pepper
1 envelope instant beef-
    flavored broth
1 package (12 ounces)
    noodles, cooked and
    drained
Chopped scallions
Toasted buttered bread
    crumbs (use in microwave
    method only)

Combine onions and butter in 2-quart microwave safe casserole. Cover and cook at 100% microwave power 5 minutes, or until very tender. Stir in sour cream, eggs, cheese, salt, pepper, and beef broth powder until well combined. Fold in noodles.

 Preheat oven to 350°F. Combo cook at 50% microwave power and 350°F 20 minutes, or until center is set and top is lightly browned. Let stand 5 minutes. Sprinkle with scallions.

 Bake at 300°F 50 to 55 minutes until center is set and top is lightly browned, rotating once. Let stand 5 minutes. Sprinkle with scallions.

 Preheat oven to 400°F. Combo cook at 50% microwave power 400°F and 20 minutes, or until center is set and top is lightly browned. Let stand 5 minutes. Sprinkle with scallions.

 Bake at 350°F 1 hour, or until center is set and top is lightly browned. Let stand 5 minutes. Sprinkle with scallions.

 Cook at 50% microwave power 23 to 25 minutes until center is set. Let stand 5 minutes. Sprinkle with bread crumbs and scallions.

The
Beauty of Bread

Banana Bread _____ 8 servings

1½ cups all-purpose flour
¾ cup firmly packed brown
    sugar
½ teaspoon baking powder
½ teaspoon baking soda
½ teaspoon salt
½ cup butter or margarine
¾ cup mashed banana
    (2 medium-size bananas)
2 eggs, beaten
½ cup chopped walnuts

Combine flour, brown sugar, baking powder, baking soda, and salt. Cut in butter until mixture is consistency of coarse crumbs. Blend banana and eggs. Add to flour mixture with the walnuts; stir until well blended. Pour into greased 8 × 4-inch loaf pan.*

 Preheat oven to 325°F. Total Cooking Time: 22 to 24 minutes. Bake at 325°F 12 minutes. Combo cook at 75% microwave power and 325°F 10 to 12 additional minutes until toothpick inserted in center comes out clean.

 Preheat oven to 300°F. Bake 45 to 55 minutes until toothpick inserted in center comes out clean, rotating once.

 Preheat oven to 375°F. Total Cooking Time: 22 to 24 minutes. Bake at 375°F 12 minutes. Combo cook at 75% microwave power and 375°F 10 to 12 additional minutes until toothpick inserted in center comes out clean.

 Preheat oven to 350°F. Bake 45 to 55 minutes until toothpick inserted in center comes out clean.

 Cook at 75% microwave power 12 to 13 minutes until top is almost dry. Let stand directly on heat proof surface 10 minutes.

* In microwave method, be sure to use a microwave safe loaf pan.

Chocolate Date Nut Loaf ⸻ 10 servings

3 squares (3 ounces)
    unsweetened chocolate
1¼ cups milk
¼ cup vegetable oil
1 egg, lightly beaten
2 cups all-purpose flour
¾ cup sugar
1 teaspoon baking powder
1 teaspoon baking soda
1 teaspoon salt
1 cup pitted chopped dates
½ cup chopped walnuts

Place chocolate in small glass mixing bowl. Cook at 75% microwave power 4 to 5 minutes until melted. Stir in milk, oil, and egg. Combine flour, sugar, baking powder, baking soda, and salt. Add flour mixture, dates, and walnuts to chocolate mixture and stir until well mixed. Pour into greased 9×5-inch loaf pan.*

MICROWAVE LAST

Preheat oven to 300°F. Total Cooking Time: 32 minutes. Bake at 300°F 25 minutes. Combo cook at 75% microwave power and 300°F 7 additional minutes, or until toothpick inserted in center comes out clean.

Preheat oven to 300°F. Bake 55 to 60 minutes until toothpick inserted in center comes out clean, rotating once.

MICROWAVE LAST

Preheat oven to 350°F. Total Cooking Time: 32 minutes. Bake at 350°F 25 minutes. Combo cook at 75% microwave power and 350°F 7 additional minutes, or until toothpick inserted in center comes out clean.

Preheat oven to 350°F. Bake 55 to 60 minutes until toothpick inserted in center comes out clean.

Cook at 75% microwave power 12 to 13 minutes until top is almost dry. Let stand directly on heat proof surface 10 minutes.

* In microwave method, be sure to use a microwave safe loaf pan.

Boston Brown Bread _____ 10 servings

1 cup yellow cornmeal
1 cup whole-wheat flour
½ cup rye flour
2 teaspoons baking soda
1½ teaspoons salt
2 cups buttermilk
⅔ cup molasses
1 cup raisins

Combine cornmeal, flours, baking soda, and salt. Stir in buttermilk, molasses, and raisins until well mixed. Pour into well greased 2-quart casserole.* Cover casserole.

 Combo cook at 50% microwave power and 250°F 20 minutes, or until toothpick inserted in center comes out clean. Invert onto serving plate and cut into wedges.

 Place casserole in larger casserole and add boiling water to come about halfway up side of covered casserole. Bake at 250°F 2 hours, or until toothpick inserted in center comes out clean. Invert onto serving plate and cut into wedges.

 Combo cook at 50% microwave power and 300°F 20 minutes, or until toothpick inserted in center comes out clean. Invert onto serving plate and cut into wedges.

 Place casserole in larger casserole and add boiling water to come about halfway up side of covered casserole. Bake at 300°F 2 hours, or until toothpick inserted in center comes out clean. Invert onto serving plate and cut into wedges.

 Cook at 75% microwave power 13 minutes. Let stand directly on heat proof surface 10 minutes. Invert onto serving plate and cut into wedges.

* In microwave method, be sure to use a microwave safe casserole.

Rye-Caraway Cheese Bread — 10 servings

2½ cups all-purpose flour
1½ cups rye flour
¼ cup firmly packed brown sugar
2 teaspoons salt
1 teaspoon caraway seed
2 packages active dry yeast
1 cup milk
¼ cup butter or margarine
½ cup shredded Cheddar cheese

Combine flours and measure 2 cups of flour mixture into mixing bowl. Add brown sugar, salt, caraway seed, and yeast. Cook milk, butter, and ⅔ cup water in glass measure at 100% microwave power about 2 minutes, or until very warm (120°F to 130°F). Pour into flour mixture and beat 5 minutes. Stir in cheese and remaining flour. Place in greased 2½-quart casserole* and turn to coat entire surface. Cover and let rise in warm place, free from draft, until almost double in bulk, about 45 minutes.

Preheat oven to 350°F. Total Cooking Time: 26 to 27 minutes. Bake at 350°F 20 minutes. Combo cook at 75% microwave power and 350°F 6 to 7 additional minutes until loaf sounds hollow when tapped on bottom. Remove from casserole immediately and cool on wire rack.

Preheat oven to 350°F. Bake 35 to 40 minutes until loaf sounds hollow when tapped on bottom, rotating once. Remove from casserole immediately and cool on wire rack.

Preheat oven to 400°F. Total Cooking Time: 26 to 27 minutes. Bake at 400°F 20 minutes. Combo cook at 75% microwave power and 400°F 6 to 7 additional minutes until loaf sounds hollow when tapped on bottom. Remove from casserole immediately and cool on wire rack.

Preheat oven to 400°F. Bake 35 to 40 minutes until loaf sounds hollow when tapped on bottom. Remove from casserole immediately and cool on wire rack.

Cook at 50% microwave power 15 to 16 minutes until top is dry. Let stand directly on heat proof surface 20 minutes. Remove from casserole and cool on wire rack.

* In microwave method, be sure to use a microwave safe casserole.

White Bread _____ 2 loaves

5½ cups all-purpose flour,
     divided
 2 tablespoons sugar
 2 teaspoons salt
 1 package active dry yeast
 1 cup milk
 ¼ cup butter or margarine
 1 egg

Combine 2 cups flour, sugar, salt, and yeast in mixing bowl. Cook milk, butter, and 1 cup water in 2-cup glass measure at 100% microwave power 2 minutes, or until very warm (120°F to 130°F). Beat into flour mixture with electric mixer until smooth. Beat 2 minutes at medium speed. Add egg and 1 cup flour. Beat 2 minutes at high speed. Stir in remaining 2½ cups flour. Place on lightly floured surface and knead about 10 minutes, or until smooth and elastic. Place in lightly greased bowl and turn to coat entire surface. Cover and let rise in warm place, free from draft, until almost double in bulk. Punch down dough and cut in half. Shape each half into loaf, pressing seams to seal. Place in 2 greased 8 × 4-inch loaf pans, tucking ends under. Let rise in warm place, free from draft, until almost double in bulk, about 45 minutes.

Preheat oven to 350°F. Total Cooking Time: 17 to 18 minutes. Bake at 350°F 10 minutes. Combo cook at 75% microwave power and 350°F 7 to 8 additional minutes until loaves are well browned and sound hollow when tapped on bottom.

Preheat oven to 325°F. Bake 30 minutes, or until loaves are well browned and sound hollow when tapped on bottom, rotating once.

Preheat oven to 400°F. Total Cooking Time: 17 to 18 minutes. Bake at 400°F 10 minutes. Combo cook at 75% microwave power and 400°F 7 to 8 additional minutes until loaves are well browned and sound hollow when tapped on bottom.

Preheat oven to 375°F. Bake 30 minutes, or until loaves are well browned and sound hollow when tapped on bottom.

Not recommended.

Corn Bread _____ 8 servings

1 cup yellow cornmeal
¾ cup all-purpose flour
1 tablespoon sugar
1 tablespoon baking powder
1 teaspoon salt
½ teaspoon baking soda
6 slices bacon, cooked and
    crumbled
1 cup buttermilk
1 egg
⅓ cup vegetable oil

Combine cornmeal, flour, sugar, baking powder, salt, and baking soda in mixing bowl. Add bacon and toss until evenly mixed. Blend buttermilk, egg, and oil until smooth. Stir into cornmeal mixture until well mixed. Pour into greased 8-inch square baking dish.*

Preheat oven to 375°F. Total Cooking Time: 15 minutes. Bake at 375°F 10 minutes. Combo cook at 75% microwave power and 375°F 5 additional minutes, or until toothpick inserted in center comes out clean.

Preheat oven to 375°F. Bake 20 to 25 minutes until toothpick inserted in center comes out clean.

Preheat oven to 425°F. Total Cooking Time: 15 minutes. Bake at 425°F 10 minutes. Combo cook at 75% microwave power and 425°F 5 additional minutes, or until toothpick inserted in center comes out clean.

Preheat oven to 425°F. Bake 20 to 25 minutes until toothpick inserted in center comes out clean.

Cook at 75% microwave power 10 minutes, or until top is dry and springs back when pressed, rotating pan once.

* In microwave method, be sure to use a microwave safe baking dish.

Cheese-Bran Muffins _____ 12 muffins

1½ cups all-purpose flour
2 tablespoons sugar
2 teaspoons baking powder
1 teaspoon salt
1¼ cups milk
1 cup wheat bran cereal
⅓ cup vegetable oil
1 egg, lightly beaten
½ cup shredded Cheddar
cheese

Combine flour, sugar, baking powder, and salt; set aside. Combine milk and cereal; let stand 5 minutes. Stir oil and egg into cereal mixture. Add cereal mixture to flour mixture; add cheese. Stir just until flour is moistened. Spoon into well greased or paper-lined muffin pans.*

MICROWAVE LAST

Preheat oven to 350°F. Total Cooking Time: 13 minutes. Bake at 350°F 10 minutes. Combo cook at 75% microwave power and 350°F 3 additional minutes, or until toothpick inserted in center comes out clean.

Preheat oven to 350°F. Bake 20 to 25 minutes until toothpick inserted in center comes out clean.

MICROWAVE LAST

Preheat oven to 400°F. Total Cooking Time: 13 minutes. Bake at 400°F 10 minutes. Combo cook at 75% microwave power and 400°F 3 additional minutes, or until toothpick inserted in center comes out clean.

Preheat oven to 400°F. Bake 20 to 25 minutes until toothpick inserted in center comes out clean.

Cook at 75% microwave power 10 to 11 minutes. Let stand directly on heat proof surface 5 minutes before serving.

* In microwave method, be sure to use a microwave safe muffin pan or custard cups.

Popovers _____ 6 servings

3 tablespoons butter or
  margarine
1 cup milk
3 eggs
½ teaspoon salt
1 cup all-purpose flour

Grease six 6-ounce custard cups. Place ½ tablespoon butter in each cup. Place cups on ceramic cooking shelf in preheated oven 5 minutes. Beat milk, eggs, and salt in small mixing bowl. Beat in flour until smooth and thickened. Pour batter into hot custard cups.

Preheat oven to 375°F. Total Cooking Time: 23 to 28 minutes. Combo cook at 75% microwave power and 375°F 3 minutes. Bake at 375°F 20 to 25 additional minutes until crisp and well browned.

Preheat oven to 350°F. Bake 45 to 50 minutes until crisp and well browned.

Preheat oven to 425°F. Total Cooking Time: 23 to 28 minutes. Combo cook at 75% microwave power and 425°F 3 minutes. Bake at 425°F 20 to 25 additional minutes until crisp and well browned.

Preheat oven to 400°F. Bake 45 to 50 minutes until crisp and well browned.

Not recommended.

Sour Cream Biscuits ⸺⸺⸺⸺ 12 biscuits

2 cups all-purpose flour
2 teaspoons baking powder
1 teaspoon salt
½ teaspoon baking soda
5 tablespoons butter or
    margarine
½ cup dairy sour cream
½ cup milk
1 scallion, sliced

Combine flour, baking powder, salt, and baking soda in bowl. Cut in butter until mixture is consistency of coarse crumbs. Blend sour cream and milk until smooth. Stir in scallion. Add sour cream mixture to flour mixture all at once, stirring just until evenly moistened. Turn onto lightly floured surface and knead 5 to 10 strokes until smooth. Roll dough to ½-inch thickness. Cut into rounds with 2½-inch biscuit cutter. Place on ungreased baking sheet.

Preheat oven to 400°F. Total Cooking Time: 10 minutes. Bake at 400°F 7 minutes. Combo cook at 50% microwave power and 400°F 3 additional minutes, or until lightly browned.

Preheat oven to 375°F. Bake 15 minutes, or until lightly browned.

Preheat oven to 450°F. Total Cooking Time: 10 minutes. Bake at 450°F 7 minutes. Combo cook at 75% microwave power and 450°F 3 additional minutes, or until lightly browned.

Preheat oven to 425°F. Bake 15 minutes, or until lightly browned.

Not recommended.

THE BEAUTY OF BREAD

Parker House Rolls _____ 2 dozen rolls

3⅓ cups all-purpose flour,
     divided
3 tablespoons sugar
1 teaspoon salt
1 package active dry yeast
½ cup milk
½ cup butter or margarine
1 egg
2 tablespoons butter or
     margarine, melted

Combine 1 cup flour, sugar, salt, and yeast in mixing bowl. Cook milk, butter, and ½ cup water in 2-cup glass measure at 100% microwave power 2 minutes, or until very warm (120°F to 130°F). Beat into flour mixture; continue to beat 2 minutes. Add egg and 1 cup flour. Beat at high speed 5 minutes. Stir in remaining 1⅓ cups flour and place on lightly floured surface. Knead about 10 minutes, or until smooth and elastic. Place in lightly greased bowl and turn to coat entire surface. Cover and let rise in warm place, free from draft, until almost double in bulk. Roll dough to ¼-inch thickness. Cut into rounds with 2½- to 3-inch biscuit cutter. Brush centers of dough rounds with melted butter, then fold in half. Place in lightly greased 9 × 13-inch baking dish. Cover and let rise in warm place, free from draft, until almost double in bulk, about 20 minutes.

Preheat oven to 375°F. Total Cooking Time: 10 minutes. Bake at 375°F 7 minutes. Combo cook at 75% microwave power and 375°F 3 additional minutes or until lightly browned.

Preheat oven to 350°F. Bake 18 to 20 minutes until lightly browned, rotating once.

Preheat oven to 425°F. Total Cooking Time: 10 minutes. Bake at 425°F 7 minutes. Combo cook at 75% microwave power and 425°F 3 additional minutes, or until lightly browned.

Preheat oven to 400°F. Bake 18 to 20 minutes until lightly browned.

Not recommended.

Filled Sticky Buns _____ 12 buns

1 pound frozen bread dough, thawed
¼ cup butter or margarine
¾ cup firmly packed brown sugar, divided
½ teaspoon cinnamon
½ cup raisins
¼ cup pancake or maple syrup

Roll bread dough on lightly floured surface into 10×18-inch rectangle. Place butter in 8- or 9-inch square microwave safe baking dish. Cook at 100% microwave power 2 minutes. Brush some of the butter over dough to within ½ inch of one long edge. Combine ½ cup brown sugar and cinnamon. Sprinkle over dough. Top with raisins. Roll, starting with edge opposite unbuttered edge. Press seam to seal. Cut roll into twelve 1½-inch slices. Stir remaining ¼ cup brown sugar and pancake syrup into butter in baking dish. Arrange rolls, cut-side down, in pan. Cover and let rise in warm place, free from draft, until almost double in bulk, about 30 minutes.

MICROWAVE LAST

Preheat oven to 375°F. Total Cooking Time: 15 minutes. Bake at 375°F 10 minutes. Combo cook at 75% microwave power and 375°F 5 additional minutes, or until browned. Let stand 5 minutes before inverting onto serving plate.

Preheat oven to 350°F. Bake 20 to 25 minutes until browned, rotating once. Let stand 5 minutes before inverting onto serving plate.

MICROWAVE LAST

Preheat oven to 425°F. Total Cooking Time: 15 minutes. Bake at 425°F 10 minutes. Combo cook at 75% microwave power and 425°F 5 additional minutes, or until browned. Let stand 5 minutes before inverting onto serving plate.

Preheat oven to 400°F. Bake 20 to 25 minutes until browned. Let stand 5 minutes before inverting onto serving plate.

Cook at 50% microwave power 11 minutes. Microwave at high 3 minutes, or until top and edges are dry. Let stand directly on heat proof surface 5 minutes before inverting.

Buttery Spoon Bread _____ 6 servings

3 cups milk
1 cup yellow corn meal
2 teaspoons sugar
1 teaspoon salt
6 tablespoons butter or
   margarine
3 eggs, lightly beaten

Combine milk and corn meal in 1½-quart microwave safe casserole. Stir in sugar and salt. Cook at 50% microwave power 8 minutes, or until corn meal mixture is very thick, stirring twice. Stir in butter until melted. Gradually beat a little hot corn meal mixture into eggs, then beat egg mixture back into corn meal mixture.

 Preheat oven to 350°F. Combo cook at 50% microwave power and 350°F 10 minutes, or until center is softly set and top is lightly browned.

 Preheat oven to 300°F. Bake 1 hour 15 minutes, or until center is softly set and top is lightly browned, rotating once.

 Preheat oven to 375°F. Combo cook at 50% microwave power and 375°F 10 to 11 minutes, or until center is softly set and top is lightly browned.

 Preheat oven to 325°F. Bake 1 hour 20 minutes, or until center is softly set.

 Cook at 75% microwave power 12 to 13 minutes until center is softly set. Let stand, covered, 10 minutes before serving.

Dumplings _____ 6 servings

1¼ cups all-purpose flour
2 tablespoon grated Parmesan
  cheese
1½ teaspoons baking powder
¾ teaspoon salt
½ teaspoon fines herbes,
  thyme, or dill
¾ cup milk
2 tablespoons vegetable oil
2 tablespoons sliced scallion

Combine flour, cheese, baking powder, salt, and fines herbes. Blend milk, oil, and scallion. Stir into flour mixture until well mixed. Spoon onto simmering Savory Chicken Stew (page 61) or other stew. Cover.

Preheat oven to 300°F. Bake at 300°F 15 minutes. Combo cook at 75% microwave power and 300°F 3 additional minutes. Remove cover and bake at 300°F 5 minutes.

Preheat oven to 300°F. Bake 10 minutes. Remove cover and bake at 300°F 5 minutes.

Preheat oven to 350°F. Bake at 350°F 15 minutes. Combo cook at 75% microwave power and 350°F 3 additional minutes. Remove cover and bake at 350°F 5 minutes.

Preheat oven to 350°F. Bake 10 minutes. Remove cover and bake 5 minutes.

Cook at 100% microwave power 5 to 6 minutes until toothpick inserted in dumplings comes out clean.

Sweet Surprises

Gingerbread _____ 8 servings

1¾ cups all-purpose flour
1½ teaspoons baking soda
  (1¼ teaspoons in
  microwave method)
1½ teaspoons ginger
 1 teaspoon cinnamon
 ¼ teaspoon ground cloves
 1 teaspoon grated orange
  zest
 ¾ cup molasses
 ⅔ cup orange juice
 6 tablespoons butter or
  margarine
 1 egg, beaten

Combine flour, baking soda, ginger, cinnamon, cloves, and orange zest. Place molasses and orange juice in large microwave safe cup. Cook at 100% microwave power 2½ minutes, or until hot. Stir in butter until melted, then quickly blend into flour mixture. Stir in egg.

MICROWAVE
LAST

Pour mixture into 9-inch square baking dish. Preheat oven to 325°F. Total Cooking Time: 19 minutes. Bake at 325°F 15 minutes. Combo cook at 75% microwave power and 325°F 4 additional minutes, or until toothpick inserted in center comes out clean. Top with whipped cream and orange peel, if desired.

Pour mixture into 9-inch square baking dish. Preheat oven to 325°F. Bake 25 to 30 minutes until toothpick inserted in center comes out clean. Top with whipped cream and orange peel, if desired.

MICROWAVE
LAST

Pour mixture into 9-inch square baking dish. Preheat oven to 350°F. Total Cooking Time: 19 minutes. Bake at 350°F 15 minutes. Combo cook at 75% microwave power and 350°F 4 additional minutes, or until toothpick inserted in center comes out clean. Top with whipped cream and orange peel, if desired.

Pour mixture into 9-inch square baking dish. Preheat oven to 350°F. Bake 25 to 30 minutes until toothpick inserted in center comes out clean. Top with whipped cream and orange peel, if desired.

Pour mixture into 8-inch square glass baking dish. Cook at 75% microwave power 7 to 8 minutes until center, top, and bottom are dry and spring back when lightly pressed. Top with whipped cream and orange peel, if desired.

Carrot Cake _____ 12 servings

2½ cups all-purpose flour
1 tablespoon baking powder
2 teaspoons cinnamon
1 teaspoon baking soda
1 teaspoon nutmeg
1 teaspoon salt
1 cup firmly packed brown sugar
¾ cup granulated sugar
¾ cup vegetable oil
4 eggs
3 cups shredded carrots (about 1 pound)
1 can (8 ounces) crushed pineapple, undrained,
1 cup chopped walnuts

Combine flour, baking powder, cinnamon, baking soda, nutmeg, and salt; set aside. Combine sugars, oil, and eggs in mixing bowl. Beat 5 minutes at high speed. Gradually add flour mixture, beating well after each addition. Fold in carrots, pineapple, and walnuts. Pour into well greased 12-cup Bundt pan.*

MICROWAVE LAST

Preheat oven to 325°F. Total Cooking Time: 35 minutes. Bake at 325°F 20 minutes. Combo cook at 75% microwave power and 325°F 15 additional minutes, or until toothpick inserted in center comes out clean. Cool in pan on wire rack 15 minutes. Invert onto serving plate and cool completely.

Preheat oven to 300°F. Bake 1 hour 5 minutes to 1 hour 10 minutes until toothpick inserted in center comes out clean. Cool in pan on wire rack 15 minutes. Invert onto serving plate and cool completely.

MICROWAVE LAST

Preheat oven to 375°F. Total Cooking Time: 35 minutes. Bake at 375°F 20 minutes. Combo cook at 75% microwave power and 375°F 15 additional minutes, or until toothpick inserted in center comes out clean. Cool in pan on wire rack 15 minutes. Invert onto serving plate and cool completely.

Preheat oven to 350°F. Bake 1 hour 5 minutes to 1 hour 10 minutes until toothpick inserted in center comes out clean. Cool in pan on wire rack 15 minutes. Invert onto serving plate and cool completely.

Cook at 75% microwave power 21 to 23 minutes until toothpick inserted in center comes out clean. Cool in pan on wire rack 15 minutes. Invert onto serving plate and cool completely.

* In microwave method, be sure to use a microwave safe Bundt pan.

Cocoa Chocolate Cake ____ Two 9-inch layers

1½ cups sugar
½ cup shortening
2 eggs
⅔ cup unsweetened cocoa
2 cups all-purpose flour
1¼ teaspoons baking soda
1 teaspoon salt
½ teaspoon baking powder
1⅓ cups milk
1 pint strawberries
2 cups heavy cream,
    whipped

Cream sugar and shortening. Beat in eggs until mixture is light and fluffy. Add cocoa and beat until smooth. Combine flour, baking soda, salt, and baking powder. Add flour mixture alternately with milk to creamed mixture. Pour into two 9-inch round cake pans.*

Preheat oven to 300°F. Total Cooking Time: 17 minutes. Bake at 300°F 12 minutes. Combo cook at 75% microwave power and 300°F 5 additional minutes, or until toothpick inserted in center comes out clean. Cool in pans on wire racks 10 minutes. Invert onto wire racks and cool completely.

Preheat oven to 300°F. Bake 25 to 30 minutes until toothpick inserted in center comes out clean. Cool in pans on wire racks 10 minutes. Invert onto wire racks and cool completely.

Preheat oven to 350°F. Total Cooking Time: 17 minutes. Bake at 350°F 12 minutes. Combo cook at 75% microwave power and 350°F 5 additional minutes, or until toothpick inserted in center comes out clean. Cool in pans on wire racks 10 minutes. Invert onto wire racks and cool completely.

Preheat oven to 350°F. Bake 25 to 30 minutes until toothpick inserted in center comes out clean. Cool in pans on wire racks 10 minutes. Invert onto wire racks and cool completely.

Cook, 1 layer at a time, at 75% microwave power 7 to 8 minutes until cake is dry in center. Cool directly on heat proof surface 10 minutes. Invert onto wire racks and cool completely.

Chop half of the strawberries; combine with 1 cup whipped cream. Spread between layers. Frost cake with remaining whipped cream. Slice remaining strawberries; arrange on cake.

* In microwave method, be sure to use microwave safe cake pans.

Sour Cream Coffeecake ———— 8 servings

¾ cup chopped walnuts
¾ cup firmly packed brown
    sugar
½ teaspoon cinnamon
1½ cups all-purpose flour
½ cup granulated sugar
1 teaspoon baking powder
½ teaspoon baking soda
¾ cup dairy sour cream
1 egg, lightly beaten
⅓ cup vegetable oil
¼ cup milk
1 teaspoon vanilla

Combine walnuts, brown sugar, and cinnamon; set aside. Combine flour, granulated sugar, baking powder, and baking soda in bowl. Stir sour cream, egg, oil, milk, and vanilla in another bowl until smooth. Add to flour mixture all at once and stir until well blended. Pour into greased 8-inch square baking dish.* Sprinkle with brown sugar mixture.

Preheat oven to 300°F. Total Cooking Time: 19 minutes. Bake at 300°F 15 minutes. Combo cook at 75% microwave power and 300°F 4 additional minutes, or until toothpick inserted in center comes out clean. Serve warm.

Preheat oven to 300°F. Bake 30 to 35 minutes until toothpick inserted in center comes out clean, rotating once. Serve warm.

Preheat oven to 350°F. Total Cooking Time: 19 minutes. Bake at 350°F 15 minutes. Combo cook at 75% microwave power and 350°F 4 additional minutes, or until toothpick inserted in center comes out clean. Serve warm.

Preheat oven to 350°F. Bake 30 to 35 minutes until toothpick inserted in center comes out clean. Serve warm.

Cook at 75% microwave power 7 minutes, or until center is dry. Let stand directly on heat proof surface 5 minutes before cutting. Serve warm.

* In microwave method, be sure to use a microwave safe baking dish.

Walnut Pumpernickel Torte _____ 8 servings

6   eggs, separated
¾   cup granulated sugar,
     divided
1   cup fine pumpernickel
     bread crumbs
1   cup finely ground walnuts
2   tablespoons all-purpose
     flour
1   teaspoon grated lemon zest
1   cup heavy cream
2   tablespoons brandy
2   tablespoons confectioners
     sugar, or to taste
½   square (½ ounce)
     semisweet chocolate,
     grated

Beat egg yolks, 1 tablespoon water, and ½ cup granulated sugar until thick and light. Fold bread crumbs, walnuts, flour, and lemon zest into yolk mixture; set aside. Beat egg whites until soft peaks form. Gradually beat in remaining ¼ cup granulated sugar and continue to beat until stiff peaks form. Stir a little of the whites into yolk mixture until smooth, then fold in remaining whites just until blended. Divide mixture between 2 greased and waxed paper-lined 9-inch round cake pans. Cook as directed below. Cool completely in pans on wire rack. Loosen cakes from side of pan and invert onto serving plate. Beat cream until thickened. Add brandy and confectioners sugar and beat until stiff peaks form. Spread half whipped cream mixture on 1 layer and top with remaining layer. Frost with remaining cream and sprinkle chocolate over top. Garnish with maraschino cherries, if desired. Chill before serving.

Preheat oven to 300°F. Total Cooking Time: 14 to 15 minutes. Combo cook at 50% microwave power and 300°F 3 minutes. Bake at 300°F 11 to 12 additional minutes until tops spring back when lightly pressed.

Preheat oven to 275°F. Bake 25 to 28 minutes until tops spring back when lightly pressed.

Preheat oven to 350°F. Total Cooking Time: 14 to 15 minutes. Combo cook at 50% microwave power and 350°F 3 minutes. Bake at 350°F 11 to 12 additional minutes until tops spring back when lightly pressed.

Preheat oven to 325°F. Bake 25 to 28 minutes until tops spring back when lightly pressed.

Not recommended.

Cinnamon Rhubarb Pie _____ 6 to 8 servings

1½ pounds rhubarb or 1 bag
    (20 ounces) frozen
    rhubarb, thawed
1½ cups sugar
  3 tablespoons cornstarch
1½ teaspoons cinnamon
  1 teaspoon grated lemon zest
  1 tablespoon butter or
    margarine
    Pastry for 2-crust 9-inch
    pie (page 158)

Wash rhubarb and cut into 1-inch pieces (5 to 6 cups). Combine sugar, cornstarch, cinnamon, and lemon zest. Add to rhubarb and toss to combine; set aside. Roll out pastry on lightly floured surface and fit into 9-inch pie plate.

MICROWAVE LAST

Spoon rhubarb mixture into pie shell and dot with butter. Roll out remaining pastry and cut into 12-inch strips. Make lattice topping over filling. Preheat oven to 375°F. Total Cooking Time: 16 to 18 minutes. Bake at 375°F 8 minutes. Combo cook at 100% microwave power and 375°F 8 to 10 additional minutes until rhubarb is tender and filling has thickened.

Spoon rhubarb mixture into pie shell and dot with butter. Roll out remaining pastry and cut into 12-inch strips. Make lattice topping over filling. Preheat oven to 350°F. Bake 40 to 50 minutes until rhubarb is tender and filling has thickened, rotating once.

MICROWAVE LAST

Spoon rhubarb mixture into pie shell and dot with butter. Roll out remaining pastry and cut into 12-inch strips. Make lattice topping over filling. Preheat oven to 425°F. Total Cooking Time: 16 to 18 minutes. Bake at 425°F 8 minutes. Combo cook at 100% microwave power and 425°F 8 to 10 additional minutes until rhubarb is tender and filling has thickened.

Spoon rhubarb mixture into pie shell and dot with butter. Roll out remaining pastry and cut into 12-inch strips. Make lattice topping over filling. Preheat oven to 400°F. Bake 40 to 50 minutes until rhubarb is tender and filling has thickened.

Not recomended.

Cheesecake _____ 12 to 16 servings

1 cup all-purpose flour
⅓ cup firmly packed brown
    sugar
⅓ cup minced walnuts
5 tablespoons butter or
    margarine
1 egg yolk
3 packages (8 ounces each)
    cream cheese, at room
    temperature
1½ cups granulated sugar
5 eggs
2 cups dairy sour cream
2 teaspoons grated lemon
    zest
2 teaspoons grated orange
    zest
3 oranges, peeled and
    sliced

Combine flour, brown sugar, and walnuts. Cut in butter until mixture is consistency of coarse crumbs. Blend egg yolk and 1 tablespoon water. Stir into flour mixture until lightly moistened. Press mixture onto bottom of greased 9-inch springform pan. (In microwave method, double first 5 ingredients, divide between 2 deep 10-inch glass pie plates and press mixture onto bottom and sides of pans.) Cook as directed below. Cool completely. Beat cream cheese and granulated sugar until smooth. Beat in eggs; blend in sour cream and zests. Pour into cooled crust. (In microwave method, divide between cooled pie crusts.)

Preheat oven to 350°F. Bake unfilled crust 8 minutes. Total Cooking Time: 35 to 40 minutes. Combo cook filled crust at 75% microwave power and 300°F 15 minutes. Bake at 300°F 20 to 25 additional minutes until center is set, rotating once. Cool completely on wire rack. Garnish with oranges. Serve chilled.

Preheat oven to 350°F. Bake unfilled crust 8 minutes. Reduce temperature to 300°F. Bake filled crust 55 to 60 minutes until center is set, rotating once. Cool completely on wire rack. Garnish with oranges. Serve chilled.

Preheat oven to 400°F. Bake unfilled crust 8 minutes. Total Cooking Time: 35 to 40 minutes. Combo cook filled crust at 75% microwave power and 350°F 15 minutes. Bake at 350°F 20 to 25 additional minutes until center is set, rotating once. Cool completely on wire rack. Garnish with oranges. Serve chilled.

Preheat oven to 400°F. Bake unfilled crust 8 minutes. Reduce temperature to 350°F. Bake filled crust 55 to 60 minutes until center is set. Cool completely on wire rack. Garnish with oranges. Serve chilled.

SWEET SURPRISES

Cook each crust at 100% microwave power 6 minutes, or until center begins to feel firm to the touch. Cook each filled crust at 75% microwave power 10 to 12 minutes until center is almost set, rotating once. Cool completely directly on heat proof surface. Garnish with oranges. Serve chilled.

Streusel Peach Pie ―――――――― 6 to 8 servings

2 pounds peaches
¾ cup granulated sugar
3 tablespoons cornstarch
1 tablespoon grated lemon
   zest
   Pastry for 1-crust 9-inch
   pie (page 158)
¾ cup rolled oats
½ cup firmly packed brown
   sugar
½ teaspoon salt
½ teaspoon cinnamon
⅓ cup butter or margarine,
   softened

Peel peaches and thinly slice. Combine granulated sugar, cornstarch, and lemon zest. Add to peaches and toss to combine. Roll out pastry on lightly floured surface and fit into 9-inch pie plate. (In microwave method, make high edge and pre-cook in microwave safe pie plate according to directions on page 158. Cool completely before filling.) Spoon peach mixture into pie shell. Combine rolled oats, brown sugar, salt, and cinnamon. Add butter and stir until crumbly

Sprinkle rolled oats mixture over peach mixture. Preheat oven to 375°F. Total Cooking Time: 14 to 16 minutes. Bake at 375°F 8 minutes. Combo cook at 100% microwave power and 375°F 6 to 8 additional minutes until peaches are tender and topping is browned and crisp. Cool slightly and serve with ice cream, if desired.

Sprinkle rolled oats mixture over peach mixture. Preheat oven to 350°F. Bake 35 to 40 minutes until peaches are tender and topping is browned and crisp, rotating once. Cool slightly and serve with ice cream, if desired.

Sprinkle rolled oats mixture over peach mixture. Preheat oven to 425°F. Total Cooking Time: 14 to 16 minutes. Bake at 425°F 8 minutes. Combo cook at 100% microwave power and 425°F 6 to 8 additional minutes until peaches are tender and topping is browned and crisp. Cool slightly and serve with ice cream, if desired.

Sprinkle rolled oats mixture over peach mixture. Preheat oven to 400°F. Bake 35 to 40 minutes until peaches are tender and topping is browned and crisp. Cool slightly and serve with ice cream, if desired.

Spoon peach mixture into pie shell and cook at 100% microwave power 5 minutes. Sprinkle with rolled oats mixture, and cook at 100% microwave power 5 minutes, or until topping is set. Cool slightly and serve with ice cream, if desired.

Sour Cream Apple Tart —————— 6 to 8 servings

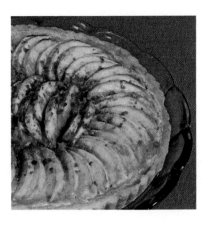

Pastry for 1-crust 9-inch
   pie (page 158)
1 pound tart cooking apples
2 tablespoons lemon juice
1 cup dairy sour cream
½ cup granulated sugar
2 eggs
2 tablespoons all-purpose
   flour
½ teaspoon cinnamon
½ teaspoon grated lemon zest
¼ cup firmly packed dark
   brown sugar

Roll out pastry and line 9-inch shallow tart pan with removable bottom.*
Pre-cook pastry as directed on page 158. Peel apples, thinly slice, and
toss with lemon juice. Arrange over pie crust in concentric circles. Blend
sour cream, granulated sugar, eggs, flour, cinnamon, and lemon zest.
Pour over apples.

Sprinkle with brown sugar. Preheat oven to 325°F. Total
Cooking Time: 18 minutes. Combo cook at 75% microwave
power and 325°F 8 minutes. Bake at 325°F 10 additional
minutes, or until set. Chill before serving.

Sprinkle with brown sugar. Preheat oven to 325°F. Bake 40 to
45 minutes until set, rotating once. Chill before serving.

Sprinkle with brown sugar. Preheat oven to 375°F. Total
Cooking Time: 18 minutes. Combo cook at 75% microwave
power and 375°F 8 minutes. Bake at 375°F 10 additional
minutes, or until set. Chill before serving.

Sprinkle with brown sugar. Preheat oven to 375°F. Bake 40 to
45 minutes until set. Chill before serving.

Cook at 75% microwave power 10 minutes. Cool slightly;
sprinkle with brown sugar. Chill before serving.

* In microwave method, use a microwave safe quiche dish.

Custard Pie _____ 6 servings

1 9-inch unbaked pie shell
  (page 158)
2 cups half-and-half or milk
½ cup sugar
3 eggs, lightly beaten
1 teaspoon grated lemon zest
¼ teaspoon salt
1 cup heavy cream, whipped
  Raspberries

(In microwave method, make high edge and pre-cook pie shell according to directions on page 158. Cool completely before filling.) Blend half-and-half, sugar, eggs, lemon zest, and salt until smooth. Pour into pie shell.

 Preheat oven to 375°F. Combo cook at 50% microwave power and 375°F 12 to 13 minutes until knife inserted in center comes out clean. Chill and serve topped with whipped cream and raspberries.

 Preheat oven to 350°F. Bake 30 to 35 minutes until knife inserted in center comes out clean, rotating once. Chill and serve topped with whipped cream and raspberries.

 Preheat oven to 425°F. Combo cook at 50% microwave power and 425°F 12 to 13 minutes until knife inserted in center comes out clean. Chill and serve topped with whipped cream and raspberries.

 Preheat oven to 400°F. Bake 30 to 35 minutes until knife inserted in center comes out clean. Chill and serve topped with whipped cream and raspberries.

 Cook at 50% microwave power 14 to 15 minutes until knife inserted in center comes out clean. Cool directly on heat proof surface. Chill and serve topped with whipped cream and raspberries.

Pecan Pie

1 9-inch unbaked pie shell (page 158)
1 cup pecan halves
3 eggs
¾ cup maple syrup or pancake syrup
½ cup dark corn syrup
½ cup firmly packed brown sugar
1½ teaspoons vanilla
¼ teaspoon salt

(In microwave method, pre-cook pie shell according to directions on page 158. Cool completely before filling.) Sprinkle pecans in pie shell. Combine eggs, maple syrup, corn syrup, brown sugar, vanilla, and salt. Pour over pecans.

 Preheat oven to 375°F. Combo cook at 50% microwave power and 375°F 13 to 14 minutes until crust is browned and knife inserted 2 inches from edge comes out clean. Cool on wire rack. Cut into wedges and serve topped with whipped cream, if desired.

 Preheat oven to 300°F. Bake 55 minutes, or until crust is browned and knife inserted 2 inches from edge comes out clean. Cool on wire rack. Cut into wedges and serve topped with whipped cream, if desired.

 Preheat oven to 425°F. Combo cook at 50% microwave power and 425°F 13 to 14 minutes until crust is browned and knife inserted 2 inches from edge comes out clean. Cool on wire rack. Cut into wedges and serve topped with whipped cream, if desired.

 Preheat oven to 350°F. Bake 55 minutes, or until crust is browned and knife inserted 2 inches from edge comes out clean. Cool on wire rack. Cut into wedges and serve topped with whipped cream, if desired.

 Cook at 75% microwave power 12 minutes, or until knife inserted 2 inches from edge comes out clean. Cool directly on heat proof surface. Cut into wedges and serve topped with whipped cream, if desired.

Peach Melba Tart _____

1 cup all-purpose flour
6 tablespoons ground almonds, divided
¾ cup sugar, divided
⅓ cup butter or margarine
1 egg yolk
1¼ pounds peaches
2 tablespoons cornstarch
½ pint fresh raspberries
1 to 2 tablespoons cherry-flavored brandy

Combine flour, 4 tablespoons almonds, and ¼ cup sugar. Cut in butter until mixture is consistency of coarse crumbs. Blend egg yolk and 1 tablespoon water. Stir into flour mixture until mixture holds together when lightly pressed. Press into 9-inch loose bottom quiche/flan pan. Peel and thinly slice peaches. Combine remaining ½ cup sugar with cornstarch. Spoon about half of the mixture over crust. Arrange peaches in concentric circles over crust. Sprinkle with remaining sugar mixture and remaining 2 tablespoons almonds.

Preheat oven to 375°F. Total Cooking Time: 25 minutes. Combo cook at 75% microwave power and 375°F 10 minutes. Bake at 375°F 15 additional minutes, or until crust is browned and peaches are tender. Cool briefly on wire rack, remove side of pan, and finish cooling. Toss raspberries with brandy and spoon over center of tart. Top with whipped cream, if desired.

Preheat oven to 350°F. Bake 35 to 40 minutes until crust is browned and peaches are tender. Cool briefly on wire rack, remove side of pan, and finish cooling. Toss raspberries with brandy and spoon over center of tart. Top with whipped cream, if desired.

Preheat oven to 425°F. Total Cooking Time: 25 minutes. Combo cook at 75% microwave power and 425°F 10 minutes. Bake at 425°F 15 additional minutes, or until crust is browned and peaches are tender. Cool briefly on wire rack, remove side of pan, and finish cooling. Toss raspberries with brandy and spoon over center of tart. Top with whipped cream, if desired.

Preheat oven to 400°F. Bake 35 to 40 minutes until crust is browned and peaches are tender. Cool briefly on wire rack, remove side of pan, and finish cooling. Toss raspberries with brandy and spoon over center of tart. Top with whipped cream, if desired.

 Not recommended.

Basic Pie Crust

Pastry for one 2-crust 9-inch pie
or two 1-crust 9-inch pie shells

2¼ cups all-purpose flour
1 teaspoon salt
¾ cup shortening
6 to 7 tablespoons ice water

Combine flour and salt in mixing bowl; add shortening and cut in with pastry blender until mixture is consistency of coarse crumbs. Add water, 1 tablespoon at a time, mixing lightly with fork until mixture binds together. For 2-crust pie, divide dough, making 1 ball of dough slightly larger than the other. For two 1-crust pies, divide dough evenly in half. Roll out dough in circle 2 inches larger than pie plate. Fit loosely into pie plate.*

To make 1-crust pie, flute edge and pre-cook (if directed in recipe) as directed below. To make 2-crust pie, fill pie shell and roll out second ball of dough in circle about 1 inch larger than pie plate. Fit over filling, press edge to seal, flute edge, and cut vents. Cook as recipe directs.

 Preheat oven to 400°F. Prick crust all over at ½-inch intervals. Total Cooking Time: 8 minutes. Bake at 400°F 5 minutes. Combo cook at 100% microwave power and 400°F 3 additional minutes, or until lightly browned and flaky.

 Preheat oven to 375°F. Line with aluminum foil and weigh down with dried beans. Bake 6 to 7 minutes. Remove foil and beans and bake 6 to 8 minutes until lightly browned.

 Preheat oven to 450°F. Prick crust all over at ½-inch intervals. Total Cooking Time: 8 minutes. Bake at 450°F 5 minutes. Combo cook at 100% microwave power and 450°F 3 additional minutes, or until lightly browned and flaky.

 Preheat oven to 425°F. Line with aluminum foil and weigh down with dried beans. Bake 6 to 7 minutes. Remove foil and beans and bake 6 to 8 minutes until lightly browned.

 Not recommended.

* If pie crust is to be used for a pie to be cooked by the microwave method, be sure to use a microwave safe pie plate.

Easy Apple Pie ⎯⎯⎯⎯⎯⎯ 6 to 8 servings

2 pounds tart cooking apples
1 cup sugar
3 tablespoons cornstarch
2 teaspoons cinnamon
¼ teaspoon ground cloves
1 teaspoon grated lemon zest
Pastry for 2-crust 9-inch
pie (page 158)
1 tablespoon milk

Peel apples and slice. Combine sugar, cornstarch, cinnamon, cloves, and lemon zest. Add apples and toss until well coated. Roll out larger half of pastry and line 9-inch pie plate. Spoon apples into pie shell and sprinkle with any remaining sugar mixture.

Roll out remaining pastry and fit over apple mixture. Flute edge and brush with milk. Preheat oven to 375°F. Total Cooking Time: 20 minutes. Bake at 375°F 10 minutes. Combo cook at 75% microwave power and 375°F 10 additional minutes, or until apples are tender.

Roll out remaining pastry and fit over apple mixture. Flute edge and brush with milk. Preheat oven to 350°F. Bake 40 to 45 minutes until apples are tender, rotating once.

Roll out remaining pastry and fit over apple mixture. Flute edge and brush with milk. Preheat oven to 425°F. Total Cooking Time: 20 minutes. Bake at 425°F 10 minutes. Combo cook at 75% microwave power and 425°F 10 additional minutes, or until apples are tender.

Roll out remaining pastry and fit over apple mixture. Flute edge and brush with milk. Preheat oven to 400°F. Bake 40 to 45 minutes until apples are tender.

Not recommended.

Walnut Raisin Cookies _____ About 5 dozen

1½ cups firmly packed brown sugar
1 cup butter or margarine, softened
2 eggs
2¾ cups all-purpose flour
2 teaspoons baking powder
1 teaspoon baking soda
1 teaspoon salt
1 teaspoon cinnamon
1 cup chopped walnuts
1 cup raisins

Cream brown sugar and butter until light. Beat in eggs until fluffy. Combine flour, baking powder, baking soda, salt, and cinnamon. Gradually beat into butter mixture. Stir in walnuts and raisins. Drop batter by rounded teaspoonfuls onto large ungreased baking sheet.*

Preheat oven to 350°F. Total Cooking Time: 8 minutes. Bake, 1 sheet at a time, at 350°F 6 minutes. Combo cook at 75% microwave power and 350°F 2 additional minutes, or until lightly browned. Carefully remove from baking sheet and cool on wire rack.

Preheat oven to 325°F. Bake 10 to 12 minutes until lightly browned. Carefully remove from baking sheet and cool on wire rack.

Preheat oven to 400°F. Total Cooking Time: 8 minutes. Bake, 1 sheet at a time, at 400°F 6 minutes. Combo cook at 75% microwave power and 400°F 2 additional minutes, or until lightly browned. Carefully remove from baking sheet and cool on wire rack.

Preheat oven to 375°F. Bake 10 to 12 minutes until lightly browned. Carefully remove from baking sheet and cool on wire rack.

Cook, 1 dish at a time, at 75% microwave power 4½ to 5 minutes until tops are dry. Let stand directly on heat proof surface 2 to 3 minutes, then remove to wire rack to cool.

* In microwave method, use a microwave safe baking dish.

Orange-Cheese Bars ———————

½ cup butter or margarine
1¼ cups all-purpose flour
¾ cup sugar, divided
¼ teaspoon salt
1 package (3 ounces) cream
    cheese
2 eggs
2 tablespoons orange juice
1 teaspoon grated orange
    zest
¼ cup ground almonds

Cut butter into flour until mixture is consistency of coarse crumbs. Stir in ¼ cup sugar and salt until well combined. Press into 9-inch square baking dish.* Cook as directed below. Cool slightly. Beat cream cheese and remaining ½ cup sugar until smooth. Beat in eggs, orange juice, and orange zest until blended. Pour over cooled crust.

 Preheat oven to 300°F. Combo cook crust at 75% microwave power and 300°F 5 minutes. Cool. Combo cook filled crust at 75% microwave power and 300°F 6 minutes, or until set. Sprinkle with almonds and cool completely in pan on wire rack. Serve at room temperature or chilled. Store in refrigerator.

 Preheat oven to 300°F. Bake crust 10 to 12 minutes until firm but not brown. Cool. Bake filled crust at 300°F 18 to 20 minutes until set. Sprinkle with almonds and cool completely in pan on wire rack. Serve at room temperature or chilled. Store in refrigerator.

 Preheat oven to 350°F. Combo cook crust at 75% microwave power and 350°F 5 minutes. Cool. Combo cook filled crust at 75% microwave power and 350°F 6 minutes, or until set. Sprinkle with almonds and cool completely in pan on wire rack. Serve at room temperature or chilled. Store in refrigerator.

 Preheat oven to 350°F. Bake crust 10 to 12 minutes until firm but not brown. Cool. Bake filled at 350°F 18 to 20 minutes until set. Sprinkle with almonds and cool completely in pan on wire rack. Serve at room temperature or chilled. Store in refrigerator.

 Cook crust at 75% microwave power 6 to 7 minutes until firm. Cool. Cook filled crust at 75% microwave power 7 to 9 minutes until set. Sprinkle with almonds and cool directly on heat proof surface. Serve at room temperature or chilled. Store in refrigerator.

* In microwave method, be sure to use a microwave safe baking dish.

Maple Walnut Cookie Bars _____ 30 bars

1½ cups all-purpose flour, divided
1 teaspoon baking powder
½ cup granulated sugar
½ cup butter or margarine
¼ cup firmly packed brown sugar
2 eggs
¾ cup pancake syrup or maple syrup
1 cup chopped walnuts
2 teaspoons vanilla

Combine 1¼ cups flour, baking powder, and granulated sugar. Cut in butter until crumbly. Press into greased 9×13-inch baking dish.* Cook as directed below; let cool 5 minutes. Blend remaining ¼ cup flour with brown sugar until smooth. Beat in eggs, syrup, walnuts, and vanilla. Pour syrup mixture into crust.

 Preheat oven to 300°F. Combo cook crust at 75% microwave power and 300°F 4 minutes. Combo cook filled crust at 50% microwave power and 300°F 7 to 8 minutes until filling is set. Cool completely. Cut into bars.

 Preheat oven to 300°F. Bake crust 10 minutes. Bake filled crust 25 to 30 minutes until filling is set. Cool completely. Cut into bars.

 Preheat oven to 350°F. Combo cook crust at 75% microwave power and 350°F 4 minutes. Combo cook filled crust at 75% microwave power and 350°F 7 to 8 minutes until filling is set. Cool completely. Cut into bars.

 Preheat oven to 350°F. Bake crust 10 minutes. Bake filled crust 25 to 30 minutes until filling is set. Cool completely. Cut into bars.

 Cook crust at 75% microwave power 6 minutes, or until dry. Cook filled crust at 75% microwave power 8 minutes, or until filling is set almost to center. Let stand directly on heat proof surface until completely cool. Cut into bars.

* In microwave method, be sure to use a microwave safe baking dish.

Date-Nut Bars ⎯⎯⎯⎯⎯⎯⎯⎯⎯⎯ 36 bars

3 eggs
¾ cup granulated sugar
¼ cup butter or margarine,
  melted
1 package (8 ounces) pitted
  dates, diced (1½ cups)
1 cup chopped walnuts
⅓ cup all-purpose flour
1 tablespoon lemon juice
½ teaspoon salt

Beat eggs and granulated sugar until light and fluffy. Fold in butter, dates, walnuts, flour, lemon juice, and salt just until well combined. Pour into greased 9 × 13-inch baking dish.*

Preheat oven to 325°F. Total Cooking Time: 14 minutes. Bake at 325°F 10 minutes. Combo cook at 75% microwave power and 325°F 4 additional minutes, or until top springs back when lightly pressed. Cool on wire rack. Sprinkle with confectioners sugar, if desired. Cut into bars.

Preheat oven to 300°F. Bake 25 to 30 minutes until top springs back when lightly pressed. Cool on wire rack. Sprinkle with confectioners sugar, if desired. Cut into bars.

Preheat oven to 375°F. Total Cooking Time: 14 minutes. Bake at 375°F 10 minutes. Combo cook at 75% microwave power and 375°F 4 additional minutes, or until top springs back when lightly pressed. Cool on wire rack. Sprinkle with confectioners sugar, if desired. Cut into bars.

Preheat oven to 350°F. Bake 25 to 30 minutes until top springs back when lightly pressed. Cool on wire rack. Sprinkle with confectioners sugar, if desired. Cut into bars.

Cook at 75% microwave power 12 to 13 minutes until set. Edges may still be slightly moist. Cool directly on heat proof surface. Sprinkle with confectioners sugar, if desired. Cut into bars.

* In microwave method, be sure to use a microwave safe baking dish.

Cream Cheese Brownies ——— 16 squares

½ cup butter or margarine
2 squares (2 ounces)
    unsweetened chocolate
1 cup granulated sugar
½ cup all-purpose flour
¼ teaspoon baking powder
2 eggs
½ cup chopped walnuts
1 package (3 ounces) cream
    cheese, at room
    temperature
¼ cup confectioners sugar
2 tablespoons butter or
    margarine, softened

Combine ½ cup butter and chocolate in glass mixing bowl. Cook at 75% microwave power 3 to 4 minutes until melted. Stir until smooth. Stir in granulated sugar, flour, baking powder, and eggs until smooth. Stir in walnuts; set aside. Blend cream cheese, confectioners sugar, and 2 tablespoons butter until smooth. Pour chocolate mixture into greased 8-inch square baking dish.* Spoon cream cheese mixture over top. Swirl gently with knife to create marbled effect.

MICROWAVE FIRST

Preheat oven to 325°F. Total Cooking Time: 11 minutes. Combo cook at 75% microwave power and 325°F 6 minutes. Bake at 325°F 5 additional minutes, or until top is shiny and springs back when pressed. Cool completely on wire rack. Cut into 2-inch squares and store in refrigerator.

Preheat oven to 300°F. Bake 30 to 35 minutes, or until top is shiny and springs back when pressed. Cool completely on wire rack. Cut into 2-inch squares and store in refrigerator.

MICROWAVE FIRST

Preheat oven to 375°F. Total Cooking Time: 11 minutes. Combo cook at 75% microwave power and 375°F 6 minutes. Bake at 375°F 5 additional minutes, or until top is shiny and springs back when pressed. Cool completely on wire rack. Cut into 2-inch squares and store in refrigerator.

Preheat oven to 350°F. Bake 25 to 30 minutes, or until top is shiny and springs back when pressed. Cool completely on wire rack. Cut into 2-inch squares and store in refrigerator.

Cook at 75% microwave power 7½ to 8 minutes until top springs back when lightly pressed near center. Let stand directly on heat proof surface 10 minutes. Cool completely on wire rack. Cut into 2-inch squares and store in refrigerator.

* In microwave method, be sure to use a microwave safe baking dish.

Very Berry Cobbler _____ 6 servings

3 cups fresh or 1 package (20 ounces) frozen blueberries, thawed
½ cup granulated sugar
1 tablespoon cornstarch
½ teaspoon grated lemon zest
1 cup all-purpose flour
1½ teaspoons baking powder
2 tablespoons brown sugar
½ teaspoon cinnamon
½ teaspoon salt
2 tablespoons butter or margarine
½ cup light cream
Ice cream

Rinse and wash berries, drain well; set aside. Combine granulated sugar, cornstarch, and lemon zest in 1½-quart microwave safe casserole. Stir in berries until well coated. Cook at 100% microwave power 8 minutes, or until simmering. Combine flour, baking powder, brown sugar, cinnamon, and salt. Cut in butter until mixture is consistency of coarse crumbs. Stir in light cream just until mixture is evenly moistened. Spoon onto simmering berry mixture.

Preheat oven to 375°F. Total Cooking Time: 11 minutes. Bake at 375°F 8 minutes. Combo cook at 75% microwave power and 375°F 3 additional minutes, or until topping is lightly browned. Cool and spoon into individual bowls. Top with ice cream.

Preheat oven to 350°F. Bake 15 to 18 minutes until topping is lightly browned and crusty. Cool and spoon into individual bowls. Top with ice cream.

Preheat oven to 425°F. Total Cooking Time: 11 minutes. Bake at 425°F 8 minutes. Combo cook at 75% microwave power and 425°F 3 additional minutes, or until topping is lightly browned. Cool and spoon into individual bowls. Top with ice cream.

Preheat oven to 400°F. Bake 15 to 18 minutes until topping is lightly browned and crusty. Cool and spoon into individual bowls. Top with ice cream.

Cook at 75% microwave power 9 to 10 minutes until topping is set. Dust with additional cinnamon for added color, if desired. Cool and spoon into individual bowls. Top with ice cream.

Cream Puffs _____ 8 servings

½ cup butter or margarine
¼ teaspoon salt
1 cup all-purpose flour
4 eggs
2 cups heavy cream
¼ cup confectioners sugar
3 tablespoons orange-
    flavored liqueur
1 package (6 ounces)
    semisweet chocolate
    pieces
1 tablespoon milk

Heat butter, salt, and 1 cup water to boiling. Remove from heat and add flour all at once, beating vigorously with wooden spoon until mixture pulls away from side of pan and forms a ball. Let stand 3 to 5 minutes to cool. Beat in eggs, one at a time, beating well after each addition, until dough is smooth and glossy. Drop dough onto large ungreased baking sheet in 8 mounds about 3 inches apart. Swirl the top of each mound with back of spoon.

 Preheat oven to 375°F. Total Cooking Time: 33 minutes. Combo cook cream puffs at 100% microwave power and 375°F 3 minutes. Bake at 375°F 30 additional minutes, or until crisp and golden. Cool completely on wire rack.

 Preheat oven to 350°F. Bake cream puffs 45 minutes. Cut a slit in side of each puff and bake 10 minutes, or until crisp and golden. Cool completely on wire rack.

 Preheat oven to 425°F. Total Cooking Time: 33 minutes. Combo cook cream puffs at 100% microwave power and 425°F 3 minutes. Bake at 425°F 30 additional minutes, or until crisp and golden. Cool completely on wire rack.

 Preheat oven to 400°F. Bake cream puffs 45 minutes. Cut a slit in side of each puff and bake 10 minutes, or until crisp and golden. Cool completely on wire rack.

 Not recommended.

Beat cream until thick. Add sugar and liqueur and beat until stiff; set aside. Melt chocolate with milk, stirring until smooth; set aside. Slice off tops of cream puffs and scoop out uncooked portion. Spoon cream mixture into puffs and replace tops. Drizzle with melted chocolate mixture. Serve immediately or refrigerate.

Caramel Custard _____ 6 to 8 servings

½ cup plus ⅓ cup sugar, divided
6 eggs
⅛ teaspoon cinnamon
3 cups half-and-half or heavy cream
2 teaspoons vanilla
1 teaspoon grated orange zest

Place ½ cup sugar in small saucepan. Heat over moderate heat until sugar melts and is lightly browned, stirring often. Pour into warm 1½-quart fluted casserole.* Tilt casserole to coat; set aside. Blend eggs, ⅓ cup sugar, and cinnamon until smooth. Beat in half-and-half, vanilla and orange zest. Pour over caramelized sugar.

 Combo cook at 40% microwave power and 275°F 18 to 20 minutes until knife inserted about 2 inches from edges comes out clean. Cool before placing in refrigerator to chill. To serve, invert onto serving plate and spoon caramel over top.

 Preheat oven to 250°F. Place casserole in larger casserole. Add hot water to come about halfway up side of casserole. Bake 1 hour 30 minutes, or until knife inserted in center comes out clean, rotating once. Cool before placing in refrigerator to chill. To serve, invert onto serving plate and spoon caramel over top.

 Combo cook at 40% microwave power and 325°F 18 to 20 minutes until knife inserted about 2 inches from edges comes out clean. Cool before placing in refrigerator to chill. To serve, invert onto serving plate and spoon caramel over top.

 Preheat oven to 300°F. Place casserole in larger casserole. Add hot water to come about halfway up side of casserole. Bake 1 hour 30 minutes, or until knife inserted in center comes out clean. Cool before placing in refrigerator to chill. To serve, invert onto serving plate and spoon caramel over top.

 Cook at 40% microwave power 23 to 25 minutes until knife inserted in center comes out clean. Cool directly on heat proof surface before chilling. To serve invert onto serving plate and spoon caramel over top.

* In microwave method, be sure to use a microwave safe casserole.

Chocolate Almond Pudding — 6 to 8 servings

½ cup butter or margarine, softened
¾ cup sugar, divided
3 squares (3 ounces) unsweetened chocolate, melted and cooled
5 eggs, separated
2 tablespoons almond-flavored liqueur
1 cup ground almonds
½ cup all-purpose flour
Chocolate sauce
1 cup heavy cream, whipped
Slivered almonds

Cream butter and ½ cup sugar until light and fluffy. Beat in chocolate. Add egg yolks, one at a time, beating well after each addition. Beat in liqueur, almonds, and flour; set aside. Beat egg whites until soft peaks form. Beat in remaining ¼ cup sugar and continue to beat until stiff peaks form. Stir large spoonful of whites into chocolate mixture, then fold in remaining whites just until combined.

 Pour chocolate mixture into greased 1½-quart heatproof bowl. Preheat oven to 325°F. Combo cook at 50% microwave power and 325°F 8 to 9 minutes until toothpick inserted in center comes out clean. Let stand 2 to 3 minutes before inverting onto serving plate. Serve warm, topped with chocolate sauce, whipped cream, and slivered almonds.

 Pour chocolate mixture into greased 1½-quart heatproof bowl. Preheat oven to 300°F. Cover bowl with aluminum foil and place in larger bowl. Add boiling water to come about halfway up side of bowl. Bake 40 minutes, or until toothpick inserted in center comes out clean. Let stand 2 to 3 minutes before inverting onto serving plate. Serve warm, topped with chocolate sauce, whipped cream, and slivered almonds.

 Pour chocolate mixture into greased 1½-quart heatproof bowl. Preheat oven to 375°F. Combo cook at 50% microwave power and 375°F 8 to 9 minutes until toothpick inserted in center comes out clean. Let stand 2 to 3 minutes before inverting onto serving plate. Serve warm, topped with chocolate sauce, whipped cream, and slivered almonds.

Pour chocolate mixture into greased 1½-quart heatproof bowl. Preheat oven to 350°F. Cover bowl with aluminum foil and place in larger bowl. Add boiling water to come about halfway up side. of bowl. Bake 40 minutes until toothpick inserted in center comes out clean. Let stand 2 to 3 minutes before inverting onto serving plate. Serve warm, topped with chocolate sauce, whipped cream, and slivered almonds.

 Pour chocolate mixture into greased 2-quart microwave safe bowl. Cook at 50% microwave power 12 to 13 minutes until set. Top will be moist. Cool directly on heatproof surface 10 minutes before inverting onto serving plate. Serve warm, topped with chocolate sauce, whipped cream, and slivered almonds.

Gingered Fruit Combo _____ 6 to 8 servings

2 tablespoons granulated
   sugar
1 tablespoon cornstarch
1/4 cup minced candied ginger
1 tablespoon lemon juice
1 can (20 ounces) pineapple
   chunks, drained,
   liquid reserved
1 cup halved and seeded red
   grapes
3 bananas
1/3 cup shredded coconut
1 tablespoon brown sugar

Combine granulated sugar and cornstarch in 1½-quart casserole.* Stir ginger, lemon juice, and ¾ cup reserved pineapple liquid into casserole. Stir until smooth. Add pineapple and grapes. Cut bananas lengthwise in half and crosswise into ½-inch pieces. Stir into pineapple mixture. Sprinkle with coconut and brown sugar.

 Preheat oven to 350°F. Combo cook at 50% microwave power and 350°F 10 minutes, or until fruit is hot and topping is lightly browned. Spoon into individual dessert dishes or serve over ice cream, if desired.

 Preheat oven to 325°F. Bake 20 to 25 minutes until fruit is hot and topping is lightly browned. Spoon into individual dessert dishes or serve over ice cream, if desired.

 Preheat oven to 400°F. Combo cook at 50% microwave power and 400°F 10 minutes, or until fruit is hot and topping is lightly browned. Spoon into individual dessert dishes or serve over ice cream, if desired.

 Preheat oven to 375°F. Bake 20 to 25 minutes until fruit is hot and topping is lightly browned. Spoon into individual dessert dishes or serve over ice cream, if desired.

 Cook at 75% microwave power 10 to 11 minutes until fruit is hot and brown sugar begins to melt. Spoon into individual dessert dishes or serve over ice cream, if desired.

* In microwave method, be sure to use a microwave safe casserole.

Caramelized Oranges ———————— 6 servings

6 large seedless oranges
1 cup sugar
1 tablespoon orange-
   flavored liqueur
   (optional)
¼ cup sliced almonds or
   shredded coconut

Peel oranges with sharp knife and remove white pith; reserve skin of 2 oranges. Place oranges in shallow baking dish;* set aside. Remove any white pith attached to reserved orange skin and cut into thin slivers, about 1-inch long. Measure ¼ cup slivered orange zest and combine with sugar and ⅓ cup water in 1-quart microwave safe casserole or glass measure. Cook at 100% microwave power 6 minutes or until mixture is syrupy. Stir in liqueur. Pour syrup over oranges. Sprinkle with almonds.

 Place rack in 4th position from bottom. Preheat broiler 3 minutes. Combo cook at 50% microwave power and broil 5 minutes, or until almonds are lightly browned and oranges are well glazed, spooning sauce over oranges once. Chill well before serving.

 Place rack in 4th position from bottom. Preheat oven to 425°F 3 minutes. Cook 7 minutes, or until almonds are lightly browned and oranges are well glazed, spooning sauce over oranges once. Chill well before serving.

 Place rack in 4th position from bottom. Preheat broiler 3 minutes. Combo cook at 50% microwave power and broil 5 minutes, or until almonds are lightly browned and oranges are well glazed, spooning sauce over oranges once. Chill well before serving.

 Place rack in 4th position from bottom. Preheat broiler 3 minutes. Broil 7 minutes, or until almonds are lightly browned and oranges are well glazed, spooning sauce over oranges once. Chill well before serving.

 Cook at 75% microwave power 3 minutes, or until oranges are well glazed, spooning sauce over oranges once. Chill well before serving.

*In microwave method, be sure to use a microwave safe baking dish.

Apricot Poached Pears ⎯⎯⎯⎯⎯ 6 servings

6 medium-size pears (about 2 pounds)
1 tablespoon lemon juice
1 cup white wine
½ cup sugar
⅓ cup chopped dried apricots
1 teaspoon grated orange zest
1 cinnamon stick
2 tablespoons toasted sliced almonds

Peel pears, leaving stems intact. Use a grapefruit knife and small spoon to hollow out core, starting from bottom of pear. Combine lemon juice and ½ cup water. Dip pears in lemon juice mixture to prevent darkening; drain well. Combine wine, sugar, apricots, orange zest, cinnamon stick, and ½ cup water in covered 2- or 2½-quart casserole.* Add pears. Cover.

 Combo cook at 75% microwave power and 300°F 13 to 15 minutes until tender. Cool pears in liquid; remove when cool. Purée cooking liquid in blender or food processor until smooth and thickened. Spoon over pears and sprinkle with almonds.

 Bake at 275°F 1 hour, or until tender. Check occasionally and add a little more water, if needed. Cool pears in liquid; remove when cool. Purée cooking liquid in blender or food processor until smooth and thickened. Spoon over pears and sprinkle with almonds.

 Combo cook at 75% microwave power and 350°F 13 to 15 minutes until tender. Cool pears in liquid; remove when cool. Purée cooking liquid in blender or food processor until smooth and thickened. Spoon over pears and sprinkle with almonds.

 Bake at 325°F 1 hour, or until tender. Check occasionally and add a little more water, if needed. Cool pears in liquid; remove when cool. Purée cooking liquid in blender or food processor until smooth and thickened. Spoon over pears and sprinkle with almonds.

 Cook at 100% microwave power 12 to 15 minutes until tender. Cool pears in liquid; remove when cool. Purée cooking liquid in blender or food processor until smooth and thickened. Spoon over pears and sprinkle with almonds.

* In microwave method, be sure to use a microwave safe casserole.

Apple Dumplings _____ 6 servings

1 cup granulated sugar
1 teaspoon cinnamon
⅛ teaspoon ground cloves
¼ teaspoon salt
6 medium-size tart apples
   Pastry for 2-crust 9-inch
      pie (page 158)
1 egg white
6 tablespoons brown sugar
6 tablespoons raisins
3 tablespoons butter or
   margarine

Combine granulated sugar, cinnamon, cloves, salt, and ¾ cup water in 9×13-inch microwave safe baking dish. Cover and cook at 100% microwave power 10 minutes, or until syrupy, stirring once. Set aside. Peel and core apples. Divide pastry into 6 equal pieces. Roll each piece on lightly floured surface into a circle big enough to enclose each apple. Beat egg white with 1 tablespoon water. Brush some of the egg white over edges of pastry dough. Place 1 apple on each pastry circle. Spoon 1 tablespoon brown sugar and 1 tablespoon raisins into each apple. Gather pastry up around top of apple, leaving a 1-inch opening on top. Brush insides of pastry at opening with remaining egg white to seal dough. Press closed lightly; place in syrup in baking dish. Top each dumpling with ½ tablespoon butter.

MICROWAVE
LAST

Preheat oven to 375°F. Total Cooking Time: 20 minutes. Bake at 375°F 5 minutes. Combo cook at 75% microwave power and 375°F 15 additional minutes, or until apples are tender and pastry is lightly browned. Serve warm, topped with syrup and whipped cream, if desired.

Preheat oven to 400°F. Bake 10 minutes. Reduce temperature to 325°F and bake 40 minutes, or until apples are tender and pastry is browned, rotating once. Serve warm, topped with syrup and whipped cream, if desired.

MICROWAVE
LAST

Preheat oven to 425°F. Total Cooking Time: 20 minutes. Bake at 425°F 5 minutes. Combo cook at 75% microwave power and 425°F 15 additional minutes, or until apples are tender and pastry is lightly browned. Serve warm, topped with syrup and whipped cream, if desired.

Preheat oven to 450°F. Bake 10 minutes. Reduce temperature to 375°F and bake 40 minutes, or until apples are tender and pastry is browned. Serve warm, topped with syrup and whipped cream, if desired.

Not recommended.

Crumble Cake _____ 12 servings

2½ cups all-purpose flour
2 teaspoons baking powder
1 teaspoon salt
1 cup butter or margarine, divided
1⅓ cups granulated sugar
3 eggs
1 cup milk
1 cup miniature semisweet chocolate pieces, divided
½ cup firmly packed brown sugar
1 cup shredded coconut
½ cup chopped walnuts

Combine flour, baking powder, and salt; set aside. Cream ¾ cup butter until smooth. Add sugar and beat until light and fluffy. Beat in eggs, one at a time, beating well after each addition. Add flour mixture to egg mixture alternately with milk, beating just until well combined. Stir in ½ cup chocolate pieces. Pour batter into greased 9 × 13-inch baking dish. Combine brown sugar and remaining ¼ cup butter until crumbly. Add coconut, walnuts, and remaining ½ cup chocolate pieces. Toss to mix; set aside.

MICROWAVE LAST

Preheat oven to 325°F. Total Cooking Time: 20 minutes. Bake at 325°F 15 minutes. Combo cook at 75% microwave power and 325°F 5 additional minutes, or until toothpick inserted in center comes out clean. Sprinkle with coconut-walnut mixture and bake at 325°F 4 to 5 minutes until topping melts and is lightly browned. Cool in pan on wire rack. Cut into squares.

Preheat oven to 300°F. Bake 40 to 45 minutes until toothpick inserted in center comes out clean, rotating once. Sprinkle with coconut-walnut mixture and bake 4 to 5 minutes until topping melts and is lightly browned. Cool in pan on wire rack. Cut into squares.

MICROWAVE LAST

Preheat oven to 375°F. Total Cooking Time: 20 minutes. Bake at 375°F 15 minutes. Combo cook at 75% microwave power and 375°F 5 additional minutes, or until toothpick inserted in center comes out clean. Sprinkle with coconut-walnut mixture and broil 3 to 4 minutes until topping melts and is lightly browned. Cool in pan on wire rack. Cut into squares.

Preheat oven to 350°F. Bake 40 to 45 minutes until toothpick inserted in center comes out clean. Sprinkle with coconut-walnut mixture and broil 3 to 4 minutes until topping melts and is lightly browned. Cool in pan on wire rack. Cut into squares.

 Not recommended.

Rum Puff Pudding _____ 6 servings

3 eggs
¾ cup sugar
¼ teaspoon salt
¾ cup half-and-half
⅔ cup all-purpose flour
½ cup butter or margarine,
     melted
¼ cup dark rum

Beat eggs, sugar, and salt about 6 minutes in electric mixer on high speed, or until light and very fluffy. Reduce speed to low and beat in half-and-half and flour just until combined. Fold in butter and rum. Pour into 1½-quart soufflé dish or casserole.

MICROWAVE
FIRST

Preheat oven to 325°F. Total Cooking Time: 20 to 25 minutes. Combo cook at 50% microwave power and 325°F 5 minutes. Bake at 325°F 15 to 20 additional minutes until pudding is lightly browned and set. Serve warm.

Preheat oven to 300°F. Bake 45 to 55 minutes until pudding is lightly browned and set. Serve warm.

MICROWAVE
FIRST

Preheat oven to 375°F. Total Cooking Time: 20 to 25 minutes. Combo cook at 50% microwave power and 375°F 5 minutes. Bake at 375°F 15 to 20 additional minutes until pudding is lightly browned and set. Serve warm.

Preheat oven to 350°F. Bake 45 to 50 minutes until pudding is lightly browned and set. Serve warm.

Not recommended.

Complete Oven Meals

Beef Goulash Menu

Beef Goulash

3 onions, sliced
¼ cup butter or margarine
2 pounds beef for stew, cut
   into 1-inch cubes
1 can (10½ ounces)
   condensed beef broth

1 green pepper, seeded and
   diced
2 to 3 tablespoons paprika
1 bay leaf

Place onions and butter in 3-quart microwave safe casserole. Cover and cook at 100% microwave power 5 minutes, stirring once. Stir in remaining ingredients and ½ cup water. Stir to combine, cover, and cook as directed on the following page.

Sauerkraut

2 pounds sauerkraut,
   drained
1 cup dry white wine
½ cup chopped onion

¼ cup firmly packed brown
   sugar
1 teaspoon caraway seed

Combine all ingredients in 1½-quart casserole.* Cover and cook as directed on the following page.

Peachy Gingerbread

1 can (16 ounces) sliced
   peaches, drained
⅓ cup firmly packed brown
   sugar

1 package (14 ounces)
   gingerbread mix

Pat peaches dry with paper towel and arrange in layer in greased 8-inch square baking dish. (In microwave method, use 2-quart microwave safe ring mold.) Sprinkle with brown sugar. Prepare gingerbread mix according to package directions and pour over peaches. Bake as directed on the following page.

Place Beef Goulash and Sauerkraut in oven. Combo cook at 100% microwave power and 300°F 15 minutes. Reduce microwave power and combo cook at 75% microwave power and 300°F 15 minutes. Place Peachy Gingerbread in oven and combo cook at 75% microwave power and 300°F 17 to 18 minutes until toothpick inserted in center comes out clean. Cool 5 minutes on wire rack before inverting onto serving dish. Test beef and remove if tender. (If not, combo cook at 75% microwave power and 300°F 5 to 10 minutes until tender.) Spoon Beef Goulash onto serving platter; surround with Sauerkraut. To serve Peachy Gingerbread, cut into squares and serve warm.

 Bake Beef Goulash at 300°F 1 hour. Place Sauerkraut in oven and bake 30 minutes. Place Peachy Gingerbread in oven and bake 35 to 40 minutes until toothpick inserted in center comes out clean. Cool in pan 5 minutes before inverting onto serving dish. Test beef and remove if tender. (If not, bake at 300°F 15 to 20 minutes until tender.) Spoon Beef Goulash onto serving platter; surround with Sauerkraut. To serve Peachy Gingerbread, cut into squares and serve warm.

 Place Beef Goulash and Sauerkraut in oven. Combo cook at 100% microwave power and 350°F 15 minutes. Reduce microwave power and combo cook at 75% microwave power and 350°F 15 minutes. Place Peachy Gingerbread in oven and combo cook at 75% microwave power and 350°F 17 to 18 minutes until toothpick inserted in center comes out clean. Cool on wire rack 5 minutes before inverting onto serving dish. Test beef and remove if tender. (If not, combo cook at 75% microwave power and 350°F 5 to 10 minutes until tender.) Spoon Beef Goulash onto serving platter; surround with Sauerkraut. To serve Peachy Gingerbread, cut into squares and serve warm.

 Bake Beef Goulash at 350°F 1 hour. Place Sauerkraut in oven and bake 30 minutes. Place Peachy Gingerbread in oven and bake 35 to 40 minutes until toothpick inserted in center comes out clean. Cool in pan on wire rack 5 minutes before inverting onto serving dish. Test beef and remove if tender. (If not, bake at 350°F 15 to 20 minutes until tender.) Spoon Beef Goulash onto serving platter; surround with Sauerkraut. To serve Peachy Gingerbread, cut into squares and serve warm.

 Cook Beef Goulash and Sauerkraut at 100% microwave power 20 minutes. Reduce power and cook at 75% microwave power 20 minutes. Place Peachy Gingerbread in oven and cook at 75% microwave power 18 to 20 minutes until dry in center. Cool directly on heat proof surface 5 minutes before inverting onto serving dish. Test beef and remove if tender. (If not, cook at 75% microwave power 5 to 10 minutes until tender.) Spoon Beef Goulash onto serving platter; surround with Sauerkraut. To serve Peachy Gingerbread, cut into squares and serve warm.

* In microwave method, be sure to use a microwave safe casserole.

Salisbury Steak Menu _____

Salisbury Steak

1 envelope onion soup mix	1½ teaspoons salt
1 tablespoon cornstarch	½ teaspoon freshly ground
1½ cups boiling water	pepper
2 pounds lean ground beef	

Combine soup mix and cornstarch in 8 × 12-inch baking dish.* Stir in 1½ cups boiling water until smooth. Combine beef, salt, and pepper. Shape into 6 small oval loaves; add to baking dish. Cook as directed on the following page.

Potatoes au Gratin

1 package (5½ ounces) au gratin potato mix	⅔ cup milk
2¼ cups boiling water	2 tablespoons butter or margarine

Combine contents of sauce mix envelope with boiling water, milk, and butter in 1½-quart casserole.* Stir until smooth. Add potatoes and stir to combine. Cook as directed on the following page.

Peas

2 packages (10 ounces each) frozen peas, partially thawed	2 tablespoons butter or margarine
	1 teaspoon salt

Place peas, butter, and salt in 1½-quart casserole.* Add ¼ cup water and cover. Cook as directed on the following page.

Apple Crisp

1½ pounds tart apples
¼ cup granulated sugar
¾ cup firmly packed brown sugar
½ cup all-purpose flour

½ cup rolled oats
½ teaspoon cinnamon
½ teaspoon nutmeg
¼ cup butter or margarine, softened

Peel and slice apples. Place in 2-quart casserole* and toss with granulated sugar. Combine brown sugar, flour, oats, cinnamon, and nutmeg. Stir in butter until mixture is consistency of coarse crumbs. Sprinkle over apples and cook as directed below.

 Preheat oven to 375°F. Place all dishes in oven. Combo cook at 100% microwave power and 375°F 13 minutes. Remove Salisbury Steak and combo cook at 100% microwave power and 375°F 2 to 3 minutes until potatoes and apples are tender and Peas are hot.

 Preheat oven to 350°F. Place Potatoes au Gratin, Peas, and Apple Crisp in oven. Bake 15 minutes. Add Salisbury Steak and bake 20 to 25 minutes until potatoes and apples are tender and beef is desired doneness.

 Preheat oven to 425°F. Place all dishes in oven. Combo cook at 100% microwave power and 425°F 13 minutes. Remove Salisbury Steak and combo cook at 100% microwave power and 425°F 2 to 3 minutes until potatoes and apples are tender and Peas are hot.

 Preheat oven to 400°F. Place Potatoes au Gratin, Peas, and Apple Crisp in oven. Bake 15 minutes. Add Salisbury Steak and bake 20 to 25 minutes until potatoes and apples are tender and beef is desired doneness.

 Place all dishes in oven. Cook at 100% microwave power 15 minutes. Remove Salisbury Steak and cook at 100% microwave power 2 minutes, or until potatoes and apples are tender and Peas are hot.

* In microwave method, be sure to use microwave safe baking dishes and casseroles.

Lasagna Menu

Lasagna

1 jar (32 ounces) spaghetti sauce	2 eggs, lightly beaten
8 to 10 lasagna noodles, uncooked	⅔ cup grated Parmesan cheese
1 container (15 ounces) ricotta cheese	1 package (8 ounces) mozzarella cheese, shredded

Combine spaghetti sauce and 1¼ cups water. Spoon about 1 cup sauce mixture into 9×13-inch baking dish.* Top with some of the noodles. Combine ricotta cheese and eggs. Spoon half of the ricotta cheese mixture over noodles; spread evenly. Sprinkle with ⅓ cup Parmesan cheese and ½ cup mozzarella cheese. Spoon about 1⅓ cups sauce mixture over cheeses. Repeat layers with some of the noodles, remaining ricotta cheese mixture, remaining Parmesan cheese, some of the mozzarella cheese, and some of the sauce mixture. Top with remaining noodles. Cover with remaining sauce and mozzarella cheese. Place baking dish in 14×20-inch oven cooking bag, fold opening under dish, and pierce top in 3 or 4 places. Cook as directed on the following page.

Artichokes

6 medium-size artichokes
   Salad dressing or melted
   butter

Lemon slices (optional)

Trim stems of artichokes even with bottom. Cut off 1 inch from top and trim tip of each leaf with scissors. Rinse and place in 3-quart casserole.* Add 1 cup water. Cover and cook as directed on the following page. Remove from oven and allow to cool. If desired, pull leaves apart in center of artichokes, pull out tiny yellow and purple leaves, and scrape out fuzzy "choke" with spoon. Rinse and invert to drain. Serve with individual small bowls of salad dressing or butter, and lemon slices.

Lemon Cake Pudding

2 eggs	½ cup lemon juice
⅔ cup sugar	¾ cup milk
¼ teaspoon salt	2 tablespoons butter or
⅓ cup all-purpose flour	margarine, melted
(⅔ cup in microwave)	
method)	

Beat eggs, sugar, and salt with electric mixer until light and fluffy. Beat in flour at low speed. Add lemon juice and milk. Fold in melted butter and pour into 1-quart casserole.* Cook as directed below.

 Combo cook Lasagna and Artichokes at 100% microwave power and 300°F 15 minutes. Place Lemon Cake Pudding in oven and combo cook at 50% microwave power and 300°F 25 minutes. Remove Artichokes; let stand to cool and serve as directed above. Remove Lasagna and let stand, covered, 10 minutes. Bake Lemon Cake Pudding at 300°F 10 minutes, or until lightly browned and set.

 Place Lasagna and Artichokes in oven. Bake at 300°F 30 minutes. Prepare Lemon Cake Pudding and place casserole in larger casserole. Add boiling water to come about halfway up side of casserole. Bake at 300°F 40 to 45 minutes until artichokes are tender and pudding is lightly browned and set. Let Lasagna stand, covered, 10 minutes before serving. Let Artichokes stand to cool; serve as directed above.

 Combo cook Lasagna and Artichokes at 100% microwave power and 350°F 15 minutes. Place Lemon Cake Pudding in oven and combo cook at 50% microwave power and 350°F 25 minutes. Remove Artichokes; let stand to cool and serve as directed above. Remove Lasagna and let stand, covered, 10 minutes. Bake Lemon Cake Pudding at 350°F 10 minutes, or until lightly browned and set.

 Place Lasagna and Artichokes in oven. Bake at 350°F 30 minutes. Prepare Lemon Cake Pudding and place casserole in larger casserole. Add boiling water to come about halfway up side of casserole. Bake at 350°F 40 to 45 minutes until artichokes are tender and pudding is lightly browned and set. Let Lasagna stand, covered, 10 minutes before serving.

 Place Lasagna and Artichokes in oven. Cook at 100% microwave power 20 minutes. Place Lemon Cake Pudding in oven and cook at 50% microwave power 30 to 35 minutes until pudding is set. Remove Artichokes; cool and serve as directed above. Let Lasagna stand, covered, 10 minutes before serving.

* In microwave method, be sure to use microwave safe baking dishes and casseroles.

Chicken Cacciatore Menu

Chicken Cacciatore

6 small whole boneless chicken breasts (about 3 pounds)
2 onions, cut into chunks
1 large green pepper, seeded and cut into chunks
½ cup dry red wine
2 tablespoons cornstarch

1 can (16 ounces) tomatoes, cut into chunks, liquid reserved
1½ teaspoons salt
1 teaspoon basil
¼ teaspoon freshly ground pepper
1 clove garlic, minced

Arrange chicken in layer in 9 × 13-inch baking dish.* Top with onions and green pepper. Stir wine and cornstarch until smooth. Blend in tomatoes with liquid, salt, basil, pepper, and garlic. Pour over chicken in baking dish. Cook as directed on the following page.

Macaroni

1 package (8 ounces) elbow macaroni
2 tablespoons butter or margarine

1 teaspoon salt
1 teaspoon oregano
½ cup grated Parmesan cheese

Combine macaroni, butter, salt, and oregano in 1½-quart casserole.* Add 3 cups hot tap water and stir. Cover and cook as directed on the following page.

Coconut Custard

4 eggs, lightly beaten	$\frac{1}{4}$ teaspoon salt
$\frac{1}{3}$ cup sugar	$\frac{1}{3}$ cup shredded coconut
$2\frac{1}{2}$ cups half-and-half or milk	Nutmeg, to taste

Beat eggs and sugar in $1\frac{1}{2}$-quart casserole.* Blend in half-and-half and salt. Sprinkle with coconut and nutmeg. Cook as directed below.

 Place all dishes in oven. Combo cook at 100% microwave power and 325°F 20 minutes. Remove cover from Macaroni, stir well, and sprinkle with cheese. Combo cook at 100% microwave power and 325°F 8 to 10 minutes until chicken is tender and custard is set 1 inch from edge. Cool Coconut Custard directly on heat proof surface.

 Cover Chicken Cacciatore with aluminum foil. Place all dishes in oven. Bake at 300°F 45 minutes. Test custard for doneness and remove when knife inserted 2 inches from edge comes out clean. Remove cover from Chicken Cacciatore and Macaroni. Stir Macaroni and sprinkle with cheese. Bake at 300°F 15 minutes, or until chicken and macaroni are tender.

 Place all dishes in oven. Combo cook at 100% microwave power and 375°F 20 minutes. Remove cover from Macaroni, stir well, and sprinkle with cheese. Combo cook at 100% microwave power and 375°F 8 to 10 minutes until chicken is tender and custard is set 1 inch from edge. Cool Coconut Custard directly on heat proof surface.

 Cover Chicken Cacciatore with aluminum foil. Place all dishes in oven. Bake at 350°F 45 minutes. Test custard for doneness and remove when knife inserted 2 inches from edge comes out clean. Remove cover from Chicken Cacciatore and Macaroni. Stir Macaroni and sprinkle with cheese. Bake at 300°F 15 minutes, or until chicken and macaroni are tender.

 Place all dishes in oven. Cook at 100% microwave power 13 minutes. Remove cover from Macaroni, stir well, and sprinkle with cheese. Cook at 100% microwave power 10 to 12 minutes until chicken is tender and custard is set 1 inch from edge. Cool Coconut Custard directly on heat proof surface.

* In microwave method, be sure to use microwave safe baking dishes and casseroles.

Spicy Pork Menu

Spicy Pork

1½ pounds boneless pork, cut
    into 1-inch cubes
1 can (16 ounces) tomatoes,
    cut into chunks
1 onion, diced
1 large green pepper, seeded
    and cut into chunks
½ cup raisins

1 teaspoon salt
¼ teaspoon freshly ground
    pepper
½ teaspoon chili powder
2 tablespoons sliced stuffed
    green olives
2 tablespoons slivered
    almonds

Combine pork, tomatoes, onion, green pepper, and raisins in 3-quart casserole. Add salt, pepper, chili powder, and ½ cup water. Stir until well combined. Cover and cook as directed on the following page.

Rice

1 cup rice
1 can (10¾ ounces)
    condensed chicken broth

Dash pepper
1 cup frozen peas

Place rice in 1½-quart casserole. Stir in chicken broth, pepper, and peas. Add 1⅓ cups hot tap water, cover, and cook as directed on the following page.

Cherry Pie

1 frozen (26 ounce) ready-
    to-bake cherry pie

Remove pie from carton and bake in metal pie plate.

Place all dishes in oven. Combo cook at 100% microwave power and 350°F 20 minutes, stirring pork and rice once. Remove Spicy Pork and Rice from oven. Bake Cherry Pie at 350°F 10 to 15 minutes until crust is well browned and filling is bubbly. Stir pork well and sprinkle with olives and almonds before serving.

 Place Spicy Pork in oven. Bake at 325°F 45 minutes. Add Rice and Cherry Pie and bake 45 to 55 minutes until pork and rice are tender, crust is well browned, and filling is bubbly. Stir pork well and sprinkle with olives and almonds before serving.

 Place all dishes in oven. Combo cook at 100% microwave power and 400°F 20 minutes, stirring pork and rice once. Remove Spicy Pork and Rice from oven. Bake Cherry Pie at 400°F 10 to 15 minutes until crust is well browned and filling is bubbly. Stir pork well and sprinkle with olives and almonds before serving.

 Place Spicy Pork in oven. Bake at 375°F 45 minutes. Add Rice and Cherry Pie and bake 45 to 55 minutes until pork and rice are tender, crust is well browned, and filling is bubbly. Stir pork well and sprinkle with olives and almonds before serving.

 Not recommended.

INDEX